THE FINANCIAL SECTOR
OF THE AMERICAN ECONOMY

EDITED BY
STUART BRUCHEY

A GARLAND SERIES

CONTAGION OF BANK FAILURES
THE RELATION TO DEPOSIT
INSURANCE AND INFORMATION

SANGKYUN PARK

GARLAND PUBLISHING, INC.
NEW YORK & LONDON
1992

Library of Congress Cataloging-in-Publication Data

Park, Sangkyun.
    Contagion of bank failures : the relation to deposit insurance and
information / Sangkyun Park.
        p.   cm. — (Financial sector of the American economy)
    ISBN 0-8153-0957-0 (acid free paper)
    1. Banks and banking—United States. 2. Bank failures—United
States. 3. Deposit insurance—United States. 4. Bank loans—United
States. I. Title. II. Series.
    HG2491.P37   1992
    332.1'0973—dc20   92-22997
                                                                    CIP

Printed on acid-free, 250-year-life paper
Manufactured in the United States of America

Preface

The United States is a center of capitalism and free enterprise. Nevertheless, the Banking Act of 1933 produced a highly protected banking system. Interest rate ceilings made it unnecessary for banks to offer high interest rates to attract depositors, and geographic barriers presented banks with relatively stable market share. Deregulation in the early 1980's restored much of the needed competition in the banking sector. However, numerous banking problems followed the deregulation of the industry, calling for further reforms. A large number of S&L institutions experienced financial difficulties in the early 1980's, and many commercial banks found their capital structure impaired in the second half of the decade.

Banking reform involves a number of important issues such as interstate banking, expansion of banking firms to other sectors, ownership of banks by commercial firms, and deposit insurance. Each of these issues contains significant implications for both economic efficiency and fairness. Due to their complicated nature, many banking issues remain unsettled. In 1991, the Bush Administration proposed a banking bill that was designed to overhaul the banking system. After heated debates, Congress failed to enact the Administration's proposals. At the time of this writing, the nation is still laboring in search of an ideal banking system.

Few people deny the benefit of competition. The key question is whether or not banking differs fundamentally from other businesses that may be smoothly governed by competition. In addressing this question, an important consideration is the vulnerability of the banking system to financial crises. Banking indeed differs from other businesses if banks, in the absence of government-backed insurance, are frequently subjected to runs regardless of their financial condition. Thus, understanding the nature and causes of financial crises should greatly enhance the ability to properly manage various banking matters. I hope that this study, which examines the vulnerability of sound banks during financial crises, helps understand the nature of financial crises and other banking issues.

Contents

CONTAGION
OF
BANK FAILURES

CHAPTER I

Introduction

Banking involves peculiar problems. The difficulties associated with banking include serious moral hazard problems, potential contagion effects of bank failures, and externalities to other sectors. These problems are widely recognized. Nevertheless, discussion of these banking problems stopped attracting public attention after the passage of the Banking Act of 1933, which imposed tight regulations on banks and established the FDIC. The public did not express concern over banking matters because of the belief that government regulation could effectively remove the difficulties associated with banking.

Despite the intervention of the government, banking problems reappeared in the 1970's and hence revived interests in banking issues. The interest rate shock at the beginning of the decade sharply increased the number of bank failures.[1] More importantly, the deregulation movement of the 1980's entailed numerous banking problems. The 1980's witnessed the ever deteriorating condition of S & L institutions and bailouts of major banks such as Continental Illinois (1984) and First Republicbank (1988).

Naturally, these developments have further stimulated the study of banking.

Experience and banking theory both indicate that the deregulation of banking with the government provision of deposit insurance can be costly because of moral hazard problems, banks' incentives to take excessive risks. This difficulty has fostered interests in competitive banking free of government intervention. Competition might eliminate moral hazard problems in banking. However, even if this were to be so, there is a fear that moral hazard may be superseded by a more serious problem, namely, the contagion of bank failures. It is a widely held belief that banking differs from other businesses, which can be smoothly governed by free market forces, due to the possibility of bank failure contagion. If a banking system without government deposit insurance is vulnerable to bank runs and can not prevent such runs from spreading, the system may be regarded as inherently unstable. Then free, competitive banking is not a feasible system. This study, which is an information based explanation of bank runs, has been motivated by this concern over possible contagion effects.

The mainstream literature of recent years [e.g., Diamond and Dybvig (1983), Waldo (1985), Postlewaite and Vives (1987)] treats the collective behavior of depositors generating bank runs as irrational and psychological. This interpretation implies that the private sector does not have any effective means to deal with bank runs. Then a banking system free of government intervention would be very vulnerable to runs, and hence inherently unstable.

This study views bank runs from a different perspective. Bank runs are disseminated not because depositors collectively behave in an irrational manner, but rather because they have information problems. Hence, the main proposition is that bank panics stem from incomplete information, more specifically, from a lack of bank-specific information. Bank panics occur when depositors, lacking bank-specific information, infer the soundness of the banks of their concern from the condition of the banking system as a whole. In other words, depositors may not panic when they believe that banks in operation have a much sounder financial structure than that of failed banks.

In a bank panic, fundamentally sound banks fail merely due to a liquidity problem arising from sudden withdrawals of deposits. Even those depositors who judge rationally may still run on solvent banks when they do not have complete information about the creditworthiness of individual banks. It is assumed that bank-specific information is costly for depositors to collect and process. Accordingly, the availability of this information critically depends upon banks' incentives to distinguish themselves in terms of financial strength.

Given the above arguments, it will be shown that competitive banking free of government intervention may not be so vulnerable to runs. When panic behavior is taken to be irrational, we cannot clearly identify the cause of bank runs. Without identifying the cause of a problem, it is almost impossible to find a solution. However, the private market should be able to find a solution when it is informed of the cause of the problem. Then such a private solution might supersede government intervention.

In Chapter II, the stability issue will be examined in detail by extensively reviewing and criticizing the existing literature.

Chapter III of this work models an economy in which individuals rationally maximize. The model shows how bank runs are disseminated, and also examines the effects of government deposit insurance. In the basic model, bank failures become contagious when depositors do not have bank-specific information. The logic is as follows. When depositors are not informed of the financial structure of individual banks, they infer the soundness of particular banks from the condition of the banking system as a whole. Obviously, the bank failure ratio indicates the strength of the banking sector. Hence, depositors estimate the risk of deposits based on the bank failure ratio, that is, they take a high failure ratio as a signal of high deposit risk. This behavior makes depositors run on banks in general upon observing a large number of bank failures.

Subsequently, the model incorporates government deposit insurance and analyzes its effects. Government provision of insurance enhances public confidence in the banking system by substantially reducing the possibility of deposit losses. However, when deposits are insured by the government, depositors are not concerned about the solvency of individual banks, and hence banks do not have incentives to demonstrate their financial strength. As a result, bank-specific information is missing.

The last section of the model explores a competitive banking system. In the absence of insurance provided by the government, banks have to prove their creditworthiness in order to attract depositors who are concerned about the security of their deposits. These efforts by banks make more bank-specific information available. The availability of bank-specific information enhances depositors' confidence in solvent banks. Then low confidence of depositors in the banking system as a whole does not necessarily lead to low confidence in particular banks.

Given the above analysis, there is a trade-off between public confidence in the banking system and the quality of information possessed by depositors when the government supplies deposit insurance. This conclusion raises the possibility that competitive banking may be a viable system after all. Solvent banks may prevent runs on themselves if they are able to provide sufficient information about their financial structure.

Chapter IV is devoted to empirical studies. Historical evidence will be furnished to support the hypothesis that the availability of information is a crucial factor determining whether or not bank failures become contagious. In several cases examined, the evidence suggests that the presence of more bank-specific information has tended to prevent or stop the contagion of bank failures.

The first empirical section compares clearing house loan certificates and equalization of reserves, and shows that clearing house loan certificates were more effective in tranquilizing bank panics because of their superiority in providing information about the quality of banks' assets. The main implication derived from the comparison is that the effectiveness of a method used to manage financial crises depended mainly on its function of providing information about the solvency of banks rather than enhancing the liquidity of banks. In making the comparison between those two devices, the section closely examines the bank panic of 1873, the only case in which equalization of reserves was implemented in U.S. history.

The second section argues that suspension of payments to terminate bank panics was a means of providing information. A very common belief is that banks were collectively suspended so that they could have time to improve their liquidity positions. This study interprets the suspension as an information verification procedure rather than a liquidity acquisition procedure. The information provision aspect was especially pronounced in the reopening procedure after the nationwide bank suspension of 1933. During the suspension, banking authorities carefully examined each bank's financial structure and permitted banks to reopen gradually, starting from the banks with the soundest financial structure. In addition, the government also endeavored to make the public understand its intention to reopen solvent banks only. In this way, the government verified that the banks that would reopen had much sounder financial structures than those of previously failed banks. The provision of information played a more important role in restoring public confidence than the supply of additional liquidity. Similar arguments can be applied to most other payment suspension cases.

The last empirical section makes a comparison among bank panics in U.S. history, and attempts to capture the relationship between the availability of bank-specific information and the magnitude of panic. In doing so, the section pays particular attention to the financial panic of 1884. The experience of 1884 was unique. Although the panic of 1884 was ignited by failures of large financial institutions, as large as those institutions that triggered other major panics, it was confined to New York City and short-lived. The interpretation is as follows. Bank runs were confined to problem banks since the financial structures of the New York banks that failed in 1884 were conspicuously different from those of other banks in the city and the rest of the country. In other words, it was relatively easy for the public to understand that the failed institutions were different from banks still in operation. Understanding the difference, depositors did not lose their confidence in other banks, and hence did not panic.

Overall, the empirical evidence examined indicates that banks or the government stopped bank runs mainly by providing information, and that bank failures were less contagious when the public was better informed. These findings highlight the importance of information about the solvency of individual banks. The importance of bank-specific information opens a possibility for solvent banks to prevent runs on themselves by proving their solvency. Given this possibility, the instability of competitive banking may not be inherent.

NOTES

1. The number and the size of banks failed were notable in the 1970's, compared with those of previous decades. The list of major banks failed includes United States National Bank in San Diego (1973), Franklin National Bank in New York (1974), Hamilton National Bank in Chattanooga (1976), and American Bank & Trust in New York (1976). In addition, the government bailed out a bank in 1971 for the first time since the passage of the Banking Act of 1933. Unity Bank of Boston was the first beneficiary of the government aid, and other banks soon received the same treatment, in particular, the Bank of the Commonwealth in Detroit (1972) and First Pennsylvania Bank in Philadelphia (1980).

CHAPTER II

Bank Runs
and the Stability of *Laissez-faire* Banking

The question of stability stems from the peculiarity of the banking business. Ordinarily, the safety of a business organization is guaranteed by its solvency. However, banks need an additional safeguard, namely, adequate liquidity. This peculiarity has been widely recognized ever since the commencement of modern banking. Adam Smith (1776) addressed banks' need of maintaining liquidity as follows:[1]

> the expenses peculiar to a bank consist chiefly in two articles: First, in the expense of keeping at all times in its coffers, for answering the occasional demands of the holders of its notes, a large sum of money, of which it loses the interest: And, secondly, in the expense of replenishing those coffers as fast as they are emptied by answering such occasional demand.

The importance of liquidity is especially pronounced when public confidence in banking is low. However, no level of liquidity is sufficient to meet excessive withdrawal demands arising out of severely impaired public confidence.[2] In discussing stability, this vulnerability of the banking sector to runs has occupied the central part of the argument.

It is generally believed that individual banks have no control over public confidence in themselves. Furthermore, once impaired confidence ignites a panic, individual banks have no safeguard against it. This logic induces the conclusion that *laissez-faire* banking is inherently unstable. An essential assumption in deriving this conclusion is that individual bank cannot by its own behavior affect the public's confidence in itself. Hence, the validity of this assumption is crucial to determine whether or not the instability is inherent. We can effectively analyze its validity by recognizing the main cause undermining public confidence in banks.

In search of the true cause, this chapter explores various opinions concerning the cause of bank runs, and examines their logical and empirical consistency. Since those arguments each contain implications regarding the stability of the banking system, this attempt should shed light on the stability of competitive banking.

1. BANK RUNS
AS A RESULT OF DEPOSITORS' EXPECTATIONS

Early writers blamed unreasoning fear of depositors for causing bank runs. According to them, the market cannot prevent financial panic since it is a "mysterious" event generated by irrational behavior of individuals. Statements made by David Ricardo (1817) epitomize this point:[3]

> Neither the Bank nor Government was at that time [1797] to blame; it was the contagion of the unfounded fears of the timid part of the community, which occasioned the run on the Bank, and it would

equally have taken place if they had not made any advances to Government, and had possessed twice their present capital.

This explanation for bank runs is problematic. In most cases, a careful examination reveals a basis for the fear of depositors.[4] Furthermore, economic theories in general do not allow the assumption of individuals' irrationality.

The argument based on irrationality was revised and elaborated as the interest in banking resurged in the 1970's. Kindleberger (1978)[5] argues that the market could act in destabilizing ways that are irrational overall, even when each participant in the market is acting rationally. According to him, this inconsistency between market and individual behavior is the fallacy of composition, in which the whole differs from the sum of its parts. On occasions, it is rational for each individual to behave in the same way as others even if his behavior in isolation does not seem rational.

Diamond and Dybvig (1983) formalize this idea in a sophisticated model.[6] Their work is probably the most influential one among recent attempts to analyze bank runs. The basic framework of their analysis has been adopted in numerous articles, e.g., Waldo (1985), Postlewaite & Vives (1987), and Diamond (1988).

Diamond and Dybvig describe the collective behavior of depositors generating bank runs as "irrational" behavior.[7] As far as the stability issue is concerned, this idea yields the same implication as Ricardo's. If running on banks is indeed irrational, the private banking sector may not have any means to prevent or to stop banking panics. This, in turn, means that banking without government intervention is inherently unstable. Given this crucial implication, it is certainly worth reviewing their work in detail and discussing the validity of it.

Diamond and Dybvig explain bank runs as a result of depositors' expectations about others' expectations. Their paper contains two major points. One concerns the optimality of the deposit contract, and the other is the existence of a bank run equilibrium. According to them, the demand deposit contract is optimal in the absence of the possibility of bank runs. Real assets being used for production are illiquid. On the part of individuals, holding illiquid assets is risky because of the probability of facing liquidity needs. This risk is not insurable due to the asymmetry of information. In other words, the liquidity need is information specific to individuals, and hence can not be verified by a third party. Given this asymmetric information, demand deposits are an optimal contractual arrangement in the sense that they in effect insure individuals' liquidity risk which is not normally insurable.

Diamond and Dybvig illustrate the existence of a bank run equilibrium using the concept of Nash equilibrium. They model a three period economy. Investment takes place in the first period, and a positive rate of return from production is realized in the third period. Individuals, who deposit their endowments in the first period, are identical *ex ante*. The difference arises in the second period when some depositors encounter liquidity needs, which are stochastic. Since the demand deposit contract is a risk sharing scheme, depositors with a liquidity need are allowed to withdraw in the second period without being penalized. A bank would not have a difficulty in meeting the withdrawal demand of depositors with immediate needs for consumption. Problems arise when early withdrawals are made by depositors who would prefer to wait until the third period were it not for the suspicion of bank failure. Such excessive withdrawals will force the bank into liquidation.

This situation is a game of expectations among depositors who do not have an immediate liquidity demand. Provided that others do not withdraw early, it is more profitable for a depositor to wait until the production activity is completed. However, if a depositor expects early withdrawals by others, he prefers to withdraw early. The reason is that the face value of deposits in the second period is greater than the *pro rata* share of the liquidation value of the bank.

The situation can be summarized by a simple pay-off matrix of a two person game.

```
                          II
            W                          NW

    W   (b, c) or              (b, c)
        (c, b)
 I

    NW  (c, b)                  (a, a)
```

where   a > b > c.

I and II stand for depositors. W and NW stand for the strategies of early withdrawal and no early withdrawal respectively. Given that the strategy of II is NW, the best response of I is NW. This combination is the desirable equilibrium which accomplishes optimality. However, when I expects that the strategy of II is W, I's best response is W. If this response becomes the strategy combination, the pay-off to I, which is either b or c, depends who is ahead in line for withdrawals. Hence, I will run to the bank as soon as he realizes that II's strategy is W, hoping that he receives b. This bank run equilibrium is even worse than an equilibrium attainable without the demand deposit contract.   Diamond and Dybvig argue that the desirable equilibrium is fragile. The good equilibrium breaks when the expectation shifts. The shift of expectations, they say, can be caused by anything (i.e., sunspot). The optimal equilibrium can hardly be guaranteed by the private market in this situation of an expectations game. Suspension of payments would not do it. Banks cannot observe the stochastic occurrence of liquidity needs, and hence do not know whether or not a depositor demanding a withdrawal has real liquidity needs. Banks serve depositors sequentially, i.e., first come, first served. In this circumstance, if banks suspend payments to stop runs, depositors with a real liquidity demand will suffer. Thus, they conclude that the suspension is not optimal.

Government provision of insurance, they argue, can substantially improve this situation. The improvement is possible by virtue of the taxing power of the government. Suppose the government is able to guarantee a nominal rate of return by taxing everybody including those who withdraw early. Then depositors do not have an incentive to withdraw early, provided that they do not have to consume immediately. For instance, the imposition of an inflation tax will make early withdrawals for the purpose of hoarding currency less attractive than receiving the guaranteed nominal sum in the future. This preference ordering is independent of the expectations about others' strategy.

This argument is a bubble explanation of bank runs; something occurs merely because it is expected to occur. The collective behavior generating the bubble is irrational. The main concern of depositors is not the solvency of a bank but the potential liquidity problem resulting from the possible behavior of others. Thus, the market fundamental, which should be the solvency of banks, does not play any role. If this analysis is valid, *laissez-faire* banking is inherently unstable. Prudent bank management would not improve the situation. Banks may secure their solvency with sufficient capital, but solvency has nothing to do with depositors' expectations. Liquidity deemed adequate in normal times would fail to meet withdrawal demands in a time of panic. Furthermore, banks, being unable to recognize the mechanism shifting depositors' expectations, cannot find any means to control depositors' behavior.

The arguments offering a bubble explanation are problematic in terms of both logical coherence and empirical consistency. The bubble explanation fails to identify the mechanism generating the bubble. The existence of a bubble may be justified by the "fallacy of composition" suggested by Kindleberger. However, the explanation remains puzzling owing to the failure to recognize the underlying forces shifting depositors' expectations. More importantly, the irrationality argument, which says that bank runs can be caused by intrinsically irrelevant variables, is not consistent with the development pattern of actual banking panics. Historically, bank runs always started on insolvent banks and spread to solvent ones. The argument that the main concern of depositors is the potential liquidity problem resulting from strategic behavior does not prepare us for this pattern in the empirical evidence. Financial panics were ignited when depositors became suspicious of the solvency of banks. Solvency is fundamentally relevant and is also under the control of banks.

2. BANK RUNS AS RATIONAL BEHAVIOR

The bubble explanation has generated numerous reactions. While many others followed the idea of Diamond and Dybvig, some authors such as Gorton (1985) and Chari & Jagannathan (1988) took information-based approaches, which explain bank runs as rational behavior. Recognizing some flaws of the bubble explanation, they attempted to remedy certain logical ambiguities and to better explain historical facts. Their attempts focus on the solvency as opposed to the liquidity of banks, and recognize incomplete information about the solvency of banks as the major problem. The main distinction between these information theoretic explanations and that of Diamond and Dybvig rests on this point. In Diamond and Dybvig's world, even an intrinsically irrelevant variable can generate bank runs. Thus the behavior of running on banks is irrational. In contrast, depositors in information-based models are rational in the sense that they utilize the best information available. Furthermore, what depositors are trying to measure is the solvency, the market fundamental, instead of the liquidity of banks.

Chari and Jagannathan seek to rationalize the analysis of Diamond and Dybvig while preserving its basic framework.[8] In particular, they focus on the process through which the equilibrium moves from a desirable equilibrium to a panic equilibrium. In their model, there are two groups of depositors whose major concern is the future returns on deposits. One group is better informed than the other about the future returns. When uninformed depositors observe a large number of other depositors withdrawing early, they conjecture that others are withdrawing not because of an early liquidity need but in anticipation of a low future return. This conjecture precipitates bank runs by inducing uninformed depositors to withdraw.

As they do in Diamond and Dybvig model, depositors act based on others' behavior. However, in this analysis, the movement to a bank run equilibrium is not an arbitrary process but a "signal extraction" process, which is rational. This logic is more coherent. Yet Chari and Jagannathan do not propose a satisfactory explanation for the contagion process running from insolvent banks to sound ones. Upon observing some depositors running on an insolvent bank, other depositors of the same bank may be alarmed and run on the bank. However, it is not clear why depositors of solvent banks take runs on insolvent banks as a signal of the insolvency of their own bank.

Gorton proposes another information-based explanation.[9] Since he employs a different framework, his approach is reviewed here in greater detail.

Gorton models a three period economy in which individuals maximize in an uncertain environment. In his world, an individual's maximization problem boils down to the selection between currency and deposits, given four crucial variables, namely, the returns from deposits, θ_1 and θ_2, and returns from currency, α_1 and α_2, in the first and second period respectively. These are stochastic variables. α_1 is known to individuals at the beginning of the first period, and α_2 becomes known at the beginning of the second period. θ_1 and θ_2 depend upon the outcome of the bank's investment which is subject to shocks. Though they are known to banks, θ_1 and θ_2 are not known to individuals and hence must be estimated. By assumption, the values of α_1 and estimated θ_1 are such that deposits are more attractive than currency holdings to individuals who maximize third period consumption. Hence, individuals' assets are kept in the form of deposits during the first period.

If depositors are completely informed, they would accurately estimate θ_2 and make a rational withdrawal decision in the second period, based on known α_2 and estimated θ_2. However, due to the lack of complete information, depositors estimate θ_2 using a "noisy indicator," which is still relevant though somewhat inaccurate. Then they make a withdrawal decision based on these estimates.

In the second period, two possible mistakes may be made by depositors because of inaccurate estimates. Individuals may mistakenly withdraw when it is more beneficial to wait until the third period (type 1 mistake). This mistake is a cause of bank runs and a source of welfare losses. The other mistake is to fail to withdraw when they should (type 2 mistake).

According to Gorton, the welfare loss owing to type 2 mistakes is not significant. The possibility of type 2 mistakes increases the expected profit of banks, provided that they can eliminate type 1 mistakes. The better prospect for profits induces more equity to be invested in the banking industry and hence makes banks safer. This effect compensates the potential welfare losses to depositors arising from the mistake of failing to withdraw when that is the right thing to do.

The possibility of making a type 1 mistake, whose effect is detrimental, can be substantially reduced by a demand deposit contract that implicitly includes provisions for suspension of payments. The demand deposit contract suggested by Gorton contains the following features. A banks may suspend payments when it desires to do so. One constraint is that suspension must be accompanied by information verification about the state of the bank's investments. The verification is assumed costly, and the cost is born by equity holders of the bank. Given these contractual arrangements, a bank cannot suspend payments to conceal insolvency. Suspension would not stop bank runs anyway if the information provided would show the bank to be insolvent. Then banks would not make such costly efforts. Based on this logic, Gorton argues, "Banks, with superior information, can signal to depositors, by suspending convertibility, that continuation of the long-term investments is mutually beneficial."[10] The main conclusion is that the demand deposit contract with the suggested features approximates the world of complete information in which optimality can be attained.

The article concentrates on the optimality of the demand deposit contract with suspension of payments, and leaves many fundamental questions concerning banking panics unanswered. Gorton uses the ambiguous term, "noisy indicator," and does not identify the nature of the information problem causing bank runs. The optimality of a deposit contract may depend on the nature of the information problem. If the "noisy indicator" is a variable which can be controlled by the government or by banks, appropriate government intervention or preventive efforts by banks would be preferred to suspension of payments after the occurrence of a panic. Even if bank panics are caused by an uncontrollable event, the solution may still depend on the nature of the event. More importantly, Gorton fails to address the issues of bank failure contagion and liquidation costs on which the peculiarity of banking rests. This failure makes his analysis less meaningful. The mistakes described by Gorton are fundamentally similar to common mistakes found in purchasing decisions of other goods. What is then special about deposit goods and associated welfare losses? In addition, Gorton does not make explicit the information verification procedure that is to accompany the suspension of convertibility. One fundamental problem associated with this negligence concerns the validity of the point that the cost of the verification is born by equity holders. When a bank becomes insolvent, the bank has nothing to lose. If the verification itself is less than perfect, an insolvent bank might well take a chance by suspending convertibility. The optimality argument, the main theme of Gorton, may be challenged unless this ambiguity is removed.

In spite of some ambiguities, these information theoretic models have made some recognizable contributions. The most significant one is the description of bank runs as rational behavior. The implication of rationality is that the private market may be able to manage bank panics as was partially demonstrated by Gorton. This thought is directly opposed to the idea that unregulated banking systems are inherently unstable.

Goodhart (1988) also recognizes bank panics as an information problem.[11] He does not discuss the issue in detail since the major concern of his work is not bank panics. Goodhart makes a brief comment on the problems associated with bank failures. According to him, a high frequency of bank failures involves the information problem of distinguishing between those causes specific to the individual failure and those common to the set of similar institutions. This information problem can in turn be the cause for a general run on bank reserves. Unlike the statements concerning the role of information found in other works, this is a very specific identification of the information problem involved in bank runs. In this respect, the interpretation of Goodhart deserves attention.

3. PRIVATE INFORMATION
AS A SOURCE OF BANKING INSTABILITY

Bruce Smith (1987) discusses the stability of laissez faire banking based on the concept of adverse selection.[12] He adopts the idea of Diamond and Dybvig that the demand deposit contract is an insurance arrangement. To this idea, he applies the results of the insurance analysis of Rothschild and Stiglitz (1976).

Adverse selection problems arise from the heterogeneity of individuals in terms of their risks, and from asymmetric information. Individuals have knowledge of their own probabilities of having bad luck, which vary from individual to individual. However, this individual-specific information cannot be observed by insurance companies. The equilibrium in this insurance market is described by a set of prices (the premium structure) that satisfies the zero profit condition of insurance companies and the insurance demand of individuals, i.e., market clearance. The conclusion by Rothschild and Stiglitz is as follows: The pooling equilibrium, offering the same premium structure to individuals with different risks, does not exist; and the separating equilibrium, characterized by different premium structures that induce each type of individual to select the one designed for his own type (self-selection), may or may not exist depending on the individual's attitude toward risk (the shape of the typical individual's indifference curve).

In the banking sector described by Smith, banks insure individuals' risk of facing a need for early consumption. In his two period model, investment takes place at the outset of the first period. For each unit invested, Q_2 units are produced in the second period, and Q_1 unit is recovered if the production is interrupted in the first period ($Q_1 < 1 < Q_2$). Some individuals are forced to consume at the end of the first period. There are two types of individuals distinguished by the probabilities to consume in the first period. The probability for type I and type II are p^1 and p^2 respectively ($p^1 < p^2$).

The banking sector is perfectly competitive. The demand deposit contract offered by banks stipulates R_1 and R_2 which are the units to be paid for each unit of deposit withdrawn in the first and second period respectively.

By the zero profit condition,

$$p \cdot Q_1 + (1-p) \cdot Q_2 = p \cdot R_1 + (1-p) \cdot R_2$$

where $\quad p = \theta \cdot p^1 + (1-\theta) \cdot p^2 \qquad$ for $\quad 0 \leq \theta \leq 1$

$\qquad \theta$ = the proportion of type 1 depositors.

In words, p is the economywide probability of early withdrawals. The left-hand side of the above equation is a bank's expected revenue when the bank invests all deposited goods for production and meets the early withdrawal demands by interrupting production. The right-hand side is the expected payment to depositors.

If depositors are composed only of type I individuals, i.e., $\theta=1$,

$$p^1 \cdot Q_1 + (1-p^1) \cdot Q_2 = p^1 \cdot R_1^1 + (1-p^1) \cdot R_2^1$$

where $\quad \underline{R}^1 = (R_1^1, R_2^1)$ is the promised return to type I depositors,
$\qquad\qquad$ contingent upon the timing of withdrawals.

If depositors are composed only of type II individuals, i.e., $\theta=0$,

$$p^2 \cdot Q_1 + (1-p^2) \cdot Q_2 = p^2 \cdot R_1^2 + (1-p^2) \cdot R_2^2$$

where $\quad \underline{R}^2 = (R_1^2, R_2^2)$ is $\underline{R}$ offered to type II depositors.

Given these zero profit conditions, the nonexistence of equilibrium can be illustrated as follows.

The possibility of no separating equilibrium is illustrated in figure A. The line labeled $\pi_i=0$ is the zero profit locus when the deposit is held only by type i. The line labeled $\pi=0$ is the zero profit locus when the composition of depositors is the same as the economywide composition, that is, θ is θ^* that is the proportion of

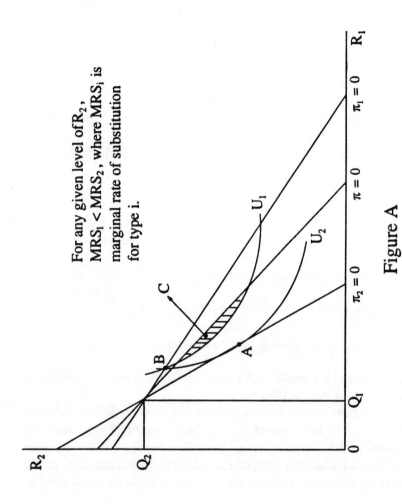

Figure A

type 1 individuals in the economy. U_i is the utility of type i. In this situation, if all banks offer deposit contracts A and B, which is consistent with the zero profit condition, A will be selected by type 1, and B will be selected by type II. The problem is that point C is definitely preferred by both types. A bank can attract both types of depositors and make a positive profit with a deposit contract offering any combination in the shaded area. Hence, the separating arrangement represented by A and B cannot be a competitive solution.

The situation of no pooling equilibrium is depicted in Figure B. Now, suppose that competition has forced banks to offer C, which is a pooling arrangement. Then the points in the shaded area are preferred only by type I. Due to "cream skimming," C cannot be a stable solution. If a bank offers D while all other banks are offering C, the bank will attract all type I depositors and enjoy a positive profit at the expense of the others. Then the latter suffer losses owing to the changed composition of depositors. If all banks offer D, both types will select D, since it is the only choice. The profit then becomes negative, so this is not an equilibrium either. Therefore, when information is asymmetric, a Nash equilibrium may fail to exist in a competitive market.

Smith concludes, "This [the failure of Nash equilibrium to exist] is the description of bank instability provided by contemporaries during all banking panics in the United States from 1857 onward." One solution suggested by Smith is the interest rate ceiling. In terms of the above analysis, no bank should be allowed to offer a rate higher than C in figure B.

Smith's claim is essentially that competition in banking is destabilizing due to the peculiar nature of the deposit contract. The nonexistence of a Nash equilibrium induces unregulated banks to offer excessively high returns to depositors. This competition makes banks collectively insolvent. Our experience of banking panics, he argues, is convincing evidence of the failure of a Nash equilibrium to exist and hence of the instability of *laissez-faire*

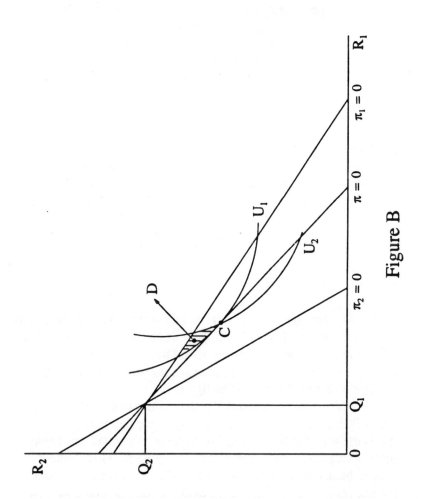

Figure B

banking. This is a strong argument that competitive banking is inherently unstable.

This analysis, however, is not consistent with our empirical findings. Historical episodes of bank panics are almost always associated with the failures of banks that had taken asset-side risks. Failed banks had offered high interest rates to depositors in order to take high asset risks with a high leverage ratio.

In Smith's analysis, if a bank takes a leading role in offering high interests to depositors, the bank can increase its profit at the expense of others. Then banks that aggressively bid up interest rates would remain solvent longer by attracting low risk depositors, while passive ones, which have fallen behind in the competition of bidding up interest rates, would be stripped of low risk depositors and become insolvent first. Empirically, banking panics were caused by the insolvency of aggressive banks that had pursued rapid expansion. We have not witnessed the collective insolvency of banks that conservatively pursued the normal profit. In general, failed banks had been managed by speculative individuals. In addition, Table 1 shows the causes of the bank failures that occurred in the years between 1865 and 1873. Major causes include excessive asset risks taken by banks, fraud, and incompetence of management. There were few cases in which banks failed purely because of general economic conditions or liquidity problems.

Therefore, it is far from clear that our experience of banking panics supports the theory that *laissez-faire* banking is inherently unstable because of the asymmetry of information concerning depositors' type.

4. INHERENTLY UNSTABLE CREDIT MECHANISM

Some writers, Mill (1848), Simons (1948), view financial crises as inevitable because of the intrinsic instability of the credit mechanism.

According to Mill, reasonable expectations of a business boom turn into a speculative bubble owing to undue extension of credit.[13] A rise of prices induces speculators to believe that the rise will continue. This over-confidence, fed by credit expansion, boosts a business upturn far above the level that could be justified on the original grounds. The burst of this speculative bubble entails a "general distrust," which is as unreasoning as the previous over-confidence. The general distrust precipitates a commercial and financial panic. This kind of panic is an inevitable result since it is the nature of the credit mechanism to accommodate speculative demand.

Simons makes similar arguments.[14] He claims that private bank credit exacerbates initial disturbances of equilibrium:[15]

> When for any reason business earnings become abnormally favorable, bank credit expands, driving sensitive product prices further out of line with sticky, insensitive costs; earnings become more favorable; credit expands farther and more rapidly; and so on and on, until costs finally do catch up, or until some speculative flurry happens to reverse the initial maladjustment. When earnings prospects are unpromising, credit contracts and earnings become still smaller and more unpromising.

Unlike expansion, the contraction can continue indefinitely unless the government intervenes. Thus, banks' ability to expand credit inevitably invites crises. Based on this logic, Simons proposes 100 percent reserve deposit banking. This is to eliminate the "perverse elasticity of credit" and to avoid economic crises. Since the elasticity of credit is in the realm of business cycle theory, it is not reviewed here. In the present context, the relevant issue is whether or not over-expansion of credit inevitably invites a financial panic by causing "unreasoning" general distrust or general insolvency. This can be answered by empirical findings. Firstly, a panic was caused not by "unreasoning" general distrust but by a fear of insolvency that had rational grounds. Without the fear of insolvency, business downturn did not produce an unreasonable demand for liquidity. Secondly, even when the solvency of the economy was undermined by over-expansion of credit, the majority of commercial and financial institutions still remained solvent. Hence, it is not justified that over-expansion of credit necessarily results in an economy-wide panic.

5. STYLIZED FACTS AND CONCLUSION

It is hard to pinpoint the ultimate causes of the financial panics that occurred in our history. They are not easily observed and may vary across different cases. Nevertheless, we can still find some common features in the history of banking panics. The analysis of such stylized facts offer a fair amount of insight into banking panics in general.

The first fact is found in the contagion pattern of banks failures. For whatever reasons, some banks become insolvent, and runs start on those insolvent banks, forcing them into liquidation. At this point, the problem is no more serious than usual bankruptcies commonly observed in other industries. In a free market economy, it is natural that some firms fail to survive competition. The real problem arises as the failures of insolvent institutions result in public suspicion of the soundness of the banking system as a whole. Such suspicion places sound banks in trouble by causing an excessive demand for liquidity. Moreover, this process is self-reinforcing due to the rising price of liquidity. This pattern allows us to infer that banking panics were triggered by fears of insolvency. If depositors were simply concerned about liquidity, they would not necessarily run on insolvent banks first.

The second notable fact is that the major banking panics in U.S. history were preceded by events which could undermine the asset position of a large number of banks (e.g. the plunge of railroad stock prices in 1857 and in 1873). Hence, banking panics occurred when the average financial condition of banks was deemed adverse. This point is supported by data. The graphs showing the ratio of banks' capital to risky assets illustrate that the ratio has rapidly declined in the periods preceding major panics, with the exception of the 1884 case (See Graph 4: Ratio of Capital to Risky Assets). The average asset positions of banks were in fact vulnerable when bank runs started. Kane (1923), who served in the Bureau of the Currency for more than 36 years, is emphatic on this point:[16]

> Every panic that has occurred during the existence of the national banking system has found its precipitating cause in some bank or business failure occurring at a time when conditions throughout the country were favorable to disturbance. The same disturbance happening at another period would probably not have extended beyond the city in which it occurred.

The significance of this finding is that depositors had rational grounds when they became suspicious of the banks' condition.

The implications of these two facts are summarized as follows. The primary concern of depositors is the solvency of banks. Accordingly, a panic is triggered by depositors' fear of insolvency. In addition, the fear has a rational basis. To run on unsound banks is rational for each and all depositors.

This rationality, however, does not justify the bank panics that trouble the whole banking system. Even during times of severe financial strain, most banks were in fundamentally sound condition. Hence, our major concern should be the protection of the sound majority. This point is well addressed by Bagehot (1873):[17]

> The amount of bad business in commercial countries is an infinitesimally small fraction of the whole business. That in a panic the bank, or banks, holding the ultimate reserve should refuse bad bills or bad securities will not make the panic really worse; the 'unsound' people are a feeble minority, and they are afraid even to look frightened

for fear their unsoundness may be detected. The great majority, the majority to be protected, are the 'sound' people, the people who have good security to offer.

The fact that the majority is "sound" magnifies the seriousness of bank failure contagion. The stability problem is pronounced when runs are disseminated from insolvent banks to sound ones. Therefore, the analysis of the stability of the competitive banking system should focus on this link connecting "ailing" banks and "healthy" ones. The question is if the private market is able to break - or at least weaken - the link that makes bank failures contagious.

Finding the best solution to a problem requires thorough understanding of the nature of the problem. What causes rational individuals, whose major concern is the solvency of banks, to run on solvent banks upon observing failures of insolvent ones? This puzzle is solved by recognizing an information problem. Depositors are primarily concerned about solvency. Yet depositors run on solvent banks because they do not know if their banks are solvent. To be more specific, the problem is that depositors can not distinguish sound banks in operation from previously failed banks.

The recent literature has failed explicitly to recognize the significance of bank-specific information. Due to this failure to identify the nature of the problem, the discussion of bank panics has concentrated on rather peripheral issues such as the necessity of maintaining high liquidity, the efficacy of suspension of payments, and the elasticity of currency. The elasticity of currency supply, in particular, occupied a central role in the older discussions before the interest in banking re-emerged in the 1970's. In effect, it was the argument for the elasticity of currency that led to the establishment of the Federal Reserve System. In discussing the crisis of 1933, Friedman and Schwartz (1863) emphasized the elasticity of currency supply and blamed the monetary authorities for their failure to provide adequate liquidity to the banking system.[18]   According to them, the panic was aggravated by a Federal Reserve system that lacked competent leadership. The Federal Reserve System failed to actively supply the needed liquidity to the banking system, while it prevented a private effort, namely, suspension of payments.

Solutions centering around the liquidity of banks, including the elasticity of currency, are treatments for symptoms rather than cures for the disease. The inadequacy of the arguments results from insufficient understanding of the nature of the problem.

This study highlights the contagion of bank failures as the major problem, and recognizes the scarcity of bank-specific information as its cause. This clarification enables us to view the stability of the competitive banking system from a different standpoint. The first significant factor is our ability to identify the cause of runs on solvent banks. It is presumably easier to eliminate a known cause of a problem than to deal with a "mysterious" phenomenon. Secondly, the main variable determining depositors' behavior is one basically under the control of banks, namely, the solvency of banks. These findings modify the idea that competitive banking is inherently unstable due to banks' inability to prevent runs. Bank runs are not a matter that is completely out of the banks' control. In addition, grasping the nature of the problem should enhance the analyses of bank panics and other issues surrounding it.

NOTES

1. Smith, Adam, *An Inquiry into the Nature and Causes of the Wealth of Nation*, Reprinted in 1976 by the University of Chicago Press, Chicago, 1776, Volume 1, p.319.
2. "Against such panics, Banks have no security, on any system; from their very nature they are subject to them, as at no time can there be in a bank, or in a country, so much specie or bullion as the monied individuals of such country have a right to demand." Ricardo, David, *On the Principles of Political Economy and Taxation*, Reprinted in 1951 by Cambridge university Press, Cambridge, 1817, pp.358, 359.
3. Ricardo (see n.2), p.359.
4. "The landing of a French frigate in one of the Welsh harbors and orders from the government to the farmers to drive their stocks into the interior, caused a run upon the Bank Of England [in 1797] which finally brought the long dreaded catastrophe of suspension of payment in coin." Conant, Charles F., *A History of Modern Banks of Issue*, Fourth Edition, The Knickerbocker Press, New York and London, 1915, p. 98. Such an unfavorable situation of the war with France should be enough to impair the confidence in the British government and creditworthiness of the Bank of England.
5. Kindleberger, Charles P., *Manias, Panics and Crashes*, Basic Books Inc., New York, 1978, Chap.3.
6. Diamond, Douglas and Dybvig, Philip, "Bank Runs, Deposit Insurance, and Liquidity," *Journal of Political Economy*, 1983.
7. Diamond and Dybvig (see n.6), p.404.
8. Chari, V. and Jagannathan, Ravi, "Banking Panics, Information, and Rational Expectations Equilibrium", *Journal of Finance*, 1988.
9. Gorton, Gary, "Bank Suspension of Convertibility," *Journal of Monetary Economics*, 1985.
10. Gorton (see n.9), p.190.
11. Goodhart, Charles, *The Evolution of Central Banks*, The MIT Press, Cambridge, Massachusetts, 1988, Chap.5.

12. Smith, Bruce, "Private Information, the Real Bills Doctrine, and Quantity Theory," *Contractual Arrangements for Intertemporal Trade*, Edited by Edward Prescott and Neil Wallace, University of Minnesota Press, Minneapolis, 1987.
13. Mill, John Stuart, *Principles of Political Economy with some of Their Applications to Social Philosophy*, Reprinted in 1902 by Longmans, Green, and Co., London, New York, and Bombay, 1848, Book III, Chap.12.
14. Simons, Henry, "A Positive Program for Laissez Faire: Some Proposals for a Liberal Economic Policy," *Economic Policy for a Free Society*, The University of Chicago press, Chicago, 1948.
15. Simons (see n.14), p.55.
16. Kane, Thomas P., *Romance and Tragedy of Banking*, Second Edition, The Bankers Publishing Co., New York, 1923, p.75.
17. Bagehot, Walter, *Lombard Street*, Reprinted in 1979 by Hyperion Press, Inc., Westport, Connecticut, 1873, p.97.
18. Friedman, Milton and Schwartz, Anna J., *Monetary History of the United States*, Princeton University Press, Princeton, 1963, pp.356, 357, 418, 419.

CHAPTER III

Bank Panics and the State of Information

The bank panic is defined in this study as runs on fundamentally sound banks. A bank is said to be fundamentally sound if: (1) the market value of the bank's assets is greater than the amount of its liabilities, without considering the liquidity premium on currency caused by the bank panic;[1] and (2) the bank has enough liquidity to meet the withdrawals arising from depositors' consumption needs, as opposed to currency hoarding demands. In a bank panic, fundamentally sound banks fail merely due to the liquidity problems caused by sudden withdrawals for the purpose of currency hoarding. This phenomenon occurs when depositors' asset preference shifts from deposits to currency holdings.

Historically, bank panics were ignited by failures of insolvent banks. This chapter develops a model focusing on this externality of bank failures. The basic model emphasizes the role of information about the financial structure of individual banks. It illustrates that bank runs spread from insolvent banks to sound ones when depositors do not have bank-specific information.

Subsequently, the model incorporates government deposit insurance and analyses its effects. The effects are two sided. The positive side is rather obvious. Depositors' confidence in the banking system as a whole is greatly enhanced when deposits are insured by the government. The negative aspect stems from the lack of incentives for banks to reveal the true strength of their balance sheets. Depositors lack bank-specific information when banks do not demonstrate their financial strength. Therefore, government deposit insurance trades bank-specific information for the systemwide confidence in banking.

The last section explores a world of competitive banking in which banks have to demonstrate their financial strength in order to attract depositors. Then the model shows that the competitive banking sector may not be so vulnerable to runs when banks provide information about their financial strength.

1. THE BASIC MODEL

This section studies a controlled environment designed to highlight the role of information in bank runs. The basic model considers neither government intervention nor any collective efforts by the private market to prevent bank runs. In this hypothetical system, banks do not make any efforts to provide financial information. In addition, it is too costly for depositors to collect and process information about the financial structure of individual banks. As a result, individuals maximize utility without financial information specific to each bank. Given this circumstance, the model shows how failures of insolvent banks cause runs on sound banks.

1.a. The Economy

The structure of the economy resembles that of Diamond and Dybvig (1983). However, in order to focus on the dissemination of bank runs rather than runs on a single bank, the model extends the time horizon to infinity and develops an overlapping generation structure. The structure is described by an infinite sequence of generations lasting two periods each. A new generation comes into existence at the beginning of every period so that two generations, the young and the old generation, co-exist at any given time.

Each generation is composed of an equal number (M) of individuals who are *ex ante* identical both within a generation and across generations **(A1)**.[2] However, some people die early at the end of the first period of their lives (type I individuals), while most people are destined to live two periods (type II individuals). This information regarding their types is revealed to individuals before the first period is over, say at the beginning of subperiod 1 (S1). Individuals have an independent probability of q $(0 < q < 1)$ of early death **(A2)**. At the outset of their lives, individuals are informed of the probability, which is the same to everybody, but not informed of their types. In this sense, they are *ex ante* identical.

In this economy, there exists one homogeneous good which can be either costlessly stored or invested in long-term production. Individuals own the storage technology, but not the production technology. Self-storage is characterized by zero rate of return and perfect liquidity. In other words, goods can be stored or removed at any time without gains or losses. In contrast, production yields a positive return, but goods invested in production are illiquid. To be specific, the rate of return from ongoing production is B_2 $(0 < B_2 < 1)$ per period. However, when investment in production is liquidated, only 1-B_1 $(0 < B_1 < 1)$ is recovered per unit invested. Liquidation always results in the cost of B_1 since long-term production is assumed not to be self-liquidating at any specified time.

This economy consists of four different economic agents: the old generation, the young generation, firms, and banks. Firms own the production technology but are not endowed with any goods. On the contrary, individuals, being endowed with goods, own only the storage technology, which is not productive.

The role of banks in this economy is to intermediate between two different generations and between individuals and producers. The costs of finding a producer and entering into a binding contract at the individual level are assumed prohibitive, i.e., greater than B_2, which is the maximum gain from production. By the same token, the cost of undertaking intergenerational transactions is also prohibitive to individuals. One possible reason for this transactions cost, which was suggested by Cass and Yaari (1966), is the "lack of sufficient overlap" between generations. In other words, it is costly for an individual to postpone his consumption until he finds another individual looking for an investment opportunity. On the other hand, banks have a superior exchange technology that enables them to intermediate at little cost.

1.b. Deposit Contract and Intermediation

Utilizing their superior exchange technology, banks offer a demand deposit contract that allows individuals to take advantage of the more productive production technology and to minimize the potential utility loss arising from early death. The demand deposit contract permits depositors to withdraw prematurely without penalty, and promises a positive return to matured deposits. This contract may be rationalized by the insurance aspect of demand deposits suggested by Diamond and Dybvig (1983).

In order to focus on individuals' maximizing behavior and its role in generating bank runs, this study adopts a partial equilibrium approach. Thus, the behavior of firms and that of banks, including the terms of deposit contract, are taken as given.

Each bank has a long-term contract with a firm, and vice versa. Given this one-to-one contract, the failure of a bank interrupts the production of only one firm, and hence does not affect the production sector as a whole. After a panic occurs, a large number of bank failures may adversely affect the entire production sector, causing deterioration of the asset positions of remaining banks. But this model, focusing on the triggering mechanism of bank runs, assumes away such feedback effects.

Deposit Contract

Time	No Bank Failure Type 1	Type 2	Bank Failure Type 1	Type 2
1	-1	-1	-1	-1
S1	1	0	$1-B_1$	$1-B_1$
2	0	1+b	0	0

A bank takes deposits from individuals and provides a firm with goods for investment. The firm promises to pay the bank B_2 unit of the good per unit borrowed at the beginning of every period subsequent to the borrowing. When needed, the bank can request the producer to liquidate the entire assets of the firm and recover $1-B_1$ unit per unit invested. Then the bank liquidates itself by distributing the recovered goods to its depositors. Banks do not have tangible capital, so depositors receive $1-B_1$ unit in the event of liquidation.

Provided that a bank remains in business, 1+b units ($0 < b < B_2$) are paid per unit deposited for a full period. If a depositor withdraws prematurely, he is repaid the principal.[3] Banks do not need to liquidate the investment to repay matured deposits. It is assumed that deposits by the young generation occur simultaneously with withdrawals by the old generation. Thus, banks use the proceeds from investment and new deposits made by the young to pay off matured deposits (principal + interest). This structure is consistent with the efficiency argument of Cass and Yaari (1966). According to them, inefficiency arises when decentralization forces people to hoard output in their first period so as to consume what they had hoarded in the second period. This hoarding results in a deadweight loss. They argue, "The only way to restore efficiency to our system is to find an arrangement whereby the savings of generation t (when it is young) are used to provide for the consumption of generation t-1 (when it is old)."

Banks understand that type 1 depositors withdraw early. In order to meet this withdrawal demand, banks hold a portion of deposits in the form of liquid assets, i.e., keep some goods in their own storage. Withdrawals take place during a period, running down the reserves of stored goods. At the beginning of the following period, banks can replenish the reserves by taking deposits from the new generation. If there is any profit from the operation in the previous period (proceeds from investments - interest payments), it is immediately consumed by the bankers, and hence are not used for increasing reserves. In addition, contract terms are such that there is no possibility of operational losses. Thus the reserve level is not affected by operational profits or losses (**A3**). In this respect, the maximization problem of banks is not endogenized.

1.c. Maximization of Individuals

An individual begins his life with an endowment of one unit of the good, which is the only resource in his life. Everybody is concerned only about consumption in the last period of his life. Hence, type 1 individuals, who are destined to die at the end of the first period, consume in the first period, while type 2 individuals living two periods postpone their consumption until the second period.

Individuals' utility function is of the following form.

$$U = U\{\delta \cdot C_I + (1 - \delta) \cdot C_{II}\} \qquad \begin{matrix} \delta = 1 \text{ with probability q} \\ \delta = 0 \text{ with probability 1-q} \end{matrix}$$

where q = the probability of early death.

C_i = the consumption in the ith period.

This utility function is state independent (**A4**), i.e., the form of utility function does not depend on the state of nature (type of individuals). Thus, the amount of consumption in each state is the sole determinant of the level of utility. In addition, individuals are assumed to be risk-neutral, i.e., $U' > 0$ and $U'' = 0$ (**A5**).

At the outset of their lives, individuals maximize utility by choosing between self-storage and deposits. In making this utility maximizing decision, they face two uncertainties: timing of consumption and the return from deposits. Assuming risk-neutrality, individuals maximize the expected amount of consumption. The probability of early death is given, but the return from deposits must be estimated. Thus, the maximizing decision critically depends upon the estimated return from deposits.

The contracted return from deposits is higher than the return from self-storage. However, due to the possibility of early withdrawals and resulting liquidity problems to be faced by banks, there exists a nontrivial probability of bank failures. Individuals estimate the probability of bank failure (e) based on the performance of banks in previous periods. Using this estimate, they determine the expected amount of future consumption from holding deposits, and select the strategy yielding the higher expected amount of consumption. In addition, should the optimal asset be deposits, individuals make a contingency plan. The plan is to withdraw at time S1 if they are found to be type I, and otherwise wait until time II.

The amount of consumption is 1 when depositors choose self-storage. From deposits, the expected amount is:

$$E(C) = e \cdot (1 - B_1) + (1 - e) \cdot q + (1 - e) \cdot (1 - q) \cdot (1 + b) \qquad \textbf{(E1)}$$

where e = the probability of bank failures in the period of the current generation's concern.

Deposit holdings entail three possible amounts of consumption depending on banks' solvency and depositors' type. If a bank fails, depositors of the bank receive $1-B_1$ unit regardless of their type.[4] Provided that a bank remains in business, it pays 1 to type I depositors, and 1+b to type II depositors. Hence, depositors consume 1 unit with the probability of $(1 - e) \cdot q$, and 1+b with the probability of $(1 - e) \cdot (1 - q)$.

Individuals hold deposits if the expected return from deposits is higher than the return from self-storage, i.e., if E(C) > 1, and rely on self-storage if E(C) $\leq$ 1.

Using E1,

$$E(C) > 1 \quad \text{when} \quad e < \{b \cdot (1 - q)\} / \{b \cdot (1 - q) + B_1\} = e^* \quad \textbf{(C1)}$$

This is the condition for individuals to choose deposits over self-storage. In words, the optimal asset of individuals shifts from deposits to self-storage when e becomes greater than e^*, resulting in an expected return from deposits lower than 1. Then bank runs occur. In this model, a large number of bank failures cause a high estimated probability of bank failures. Hence, bank runs are triggered by a large number of bank failures.

1.d. The Banking Sector and the Distribution of Withdrawals

The banking sector consists of N banks of identical size (**A6**). They have the same number of depositors and the same amount of deposits. Although the size of banks is identical, the financial structure differs across banks. Banks are classified into two types by their financial structure. One is conservative banks with sound financial structure (type A), and the other is speculative banks with problematic financial structure (type B). The crucial distinction in this model is that type A banks maintain a higher level of reserves than that of type B.[5] For analytical convenience, it is assumed that the economy starts each period with the same number of banks, N ($N = N_A + N_B$) (**A7**). Banks failed in the previous period are replaced by an equal number of new banks at the beginning of each period.

Banks face stochastic withdrawals due to the uncertainty associated with depositors' type. Since individuals have an independent probability of q to be type I (by A2), every depositor of a bank has the probability of q to withdraw early. Given the assumption of independence, the number of type 1 depositors (early withdrawer) of a bank, m^I, is binomially distributed with parameters (n = m, p = q), where m is the number of depositors per bank, M/N.

$$m^I \sim b(m, q)$$

Hence, $E(m^I) = q \cdot m$

$$Var.(m^I) = q \cdot (1 - q) \cdot m$$

Since everybody is endowed with one unit of the good, the amount of deposit is 1 per depositor. Thus the distribution of stochastic withdrawals faced by a bank is equal to the distribution of m^I.

In addition, the assumptions of independent probability and identical size of banks (A2 and A6) lead us to conclude that banks face stochastic withdrawals that are independently and identically distributed (**C2**). Each bank has the same number of identical depositors. Thus, the distribution of withdrawals is the same for all banks. Since the probability of becoming type I is independent, the distribution of withdrawals is also independent across banks.

A bank fails if withdrawals exceed its reserve holdings. Out of m units of deposits, banks keep $R \cdot m$ units in their storage as reserves, and invest the rest in production. Due to the long-term nature of the investment, no bank can withstand a run. Ignoring for the moment the possibility of bank runs and considering only withdrawals due to premature death of depositors, a bank fails at time S1 if stochastic withdrawals exceed its reserve holdings. The probability that a type j bank fails in this manner is:

$$p_j = \sum_{i=R_j \cdot m+1}^{m} \binom{m}{i} q^i \cdot (1-q)^{m-i} \qquad j=A, B$$

where R_j is the reserve ratio for type j bank.

This is the probability that the number of type 1 depositors of a bank turns out to be greater than $R \cdot m$.

Since the distribution of withdrawals is the same as the distribution of the number of type 1 individuals, withdrawals exceed reserve holdings when more than $R \cdot m$ depositors become type 1. This probability is independent across banks since each bank faces an independent distribution of stochastic withdrawals. Apparently,

$$p_A < p_B \quad \text{since} \quad R_A > R_B$$

In addition, provided that bank runs did not occur, each bank starts a period with a constant amount of deposits and reserves (By A1 and A3). Hence, p_A and p_B remain constant over time.

Given these results, the number of type j (j = A, B) bank failures (n_j) resulting from stochastic withdrawals is binomially distributed:

$$n_j \sim b(N_j, p_j)$$

where N_j = the total number of type j banks.

p_j = the probability of the failure of a type j bank.

Furthermore, these distributions are independent of each other (**C3**). Every bank regardless of its type has an independent probability of failure. Accordingly, the number of type A bank failures is independent of the number of type B bank failures.

Given the independence, the expected total number of failures increases with the proportion of type B banks. Hence, a large number of failures signals a high proportion of speculative banks.

1.e. The Estimation of Risks (Determination of e)

Due to the lack of bank specific information, depositors do not know the type of their banks. As a result, they are unable to measure the probability of failure specific to each bank. Depositors estimate the economywide proportion of type B (speculative) banks, which is denoted as θ. Then they use the estimate of θ to infer the probability that a particular bank fails.

The proportion θ is a fixed number and not known to depositors. They believe that θ is either θ_1 or θ_2 ($\theta_1 < \theta_2$) and assign a probability to each value of θ.[6] The depositors' estimate at time t is that:

$$P(\theta = \theta_1) = x_t$$

$$P(\theta = \theta_2) = 1 - x_t$$

The estimate of θ is a crucial component in determining the perceived deposit risk. If the estimate at time t is θ_2, i.e., $x_t = 0$, depositors prefer self-storage to deposits, while the estimated θ value of θ_1 results in deposits dominating self-storage (**A8**). Depositors revise x_t using a Bayesian inference rule as new information arrives. In other words, they observe the number of bank failures each period, and utilize this information in estimating the proportion of speculative banks.

In addition, the following information is available to the public:

1) The reserve ratios of the two different types of banks,
R_A and R_B.

Although depositors are not informed of the financial structure specific to each bank, they understand that some banks (speculative ones) maintain a low level of reserves relative to others (conservative ones).

2) The density function of early withdrawals faced by banks.

In other word, depositors understand the nature of stochastic withdrawals.

Using (1) and (2), the public correctly calculates bank failure probabilities of each type, p_A and p_B. These are probabilities that stochastic withdrawals exceed the reserve holdings of a bank. Given p_A and p_B,

$$e_t = (1 - \theta_t) \cdot p_A + \theta_t \cdot p_B \qquad \text{(E2)}$$

where e_t = probability that a bank fails at time t.

θ_t = estimated value of θ at time t.

Banks are of identical size, and their types cannot be identified by depositors. Hence, for a depositor, the probability of his bank being type B is θ. Accordingly, the probability that his bank fails is the weighted average of p_A and p_B, where the weights are the proportion of each type of banks, $1-\theta$ and θ.

At the beginning of each period, individuals estimate the distribution of θ utilizing their knowledge of the distributional form. Given the distribution assumed previously,

$$\theta_t = x_t \cdot \theta_1 + (1 - x_t) \cdot \theta_2 \qquad \text{(E3)}$$

That is, depositors use the mean value of the distribution of θ estimated at time t. This decision rule, as suggested above, leads to the same qualitative results for this analysis also when a more complicated distribution of θ is assumed, and hence justifies the simple distribution of θ assumed above.

The distribution is estimated by a Bayesian inference rule. Depositors infer the distribution based on the number of bank failures that have occurred in previous periods. Since θ takes one of two values, θ_1 or θ_2, the entire distribution of θ is summarized by x_t. Once x_t is determined, the probability that θ equals θ_2 is automatically $1-x_t$.

Algebraically, the Bayesian posterior probability that θ equals θ_1 is:

$$x_t = \{L(n_{t-1} \mid \theta_1) \cdot x_{t-1}\} /$$

$$\{L(n_{t-1} \mid \theta_1) \cdot x_{t-1} + L(n_{t-1} \mid \theta_2) \cdot (1-x_{t-1})\} \qquad \textbf{(E4)}$$

where n_{t-1} = the number of failures at time t-1.

$L(n \mid \theta_i)$ = the likelihood of observing n given $\theta = \theta_i$.

x_{t-1} = x estimated on the basis of the information at time t-1. This is the prior belief held by generation t.

In words, depositors revise their estimate of the distribution of θ at the beginning of each period utilizing the current information, namely, the number of bank failures in the previous period. When depositors measure deposit risk in this manner, failures of individual banks cause depositors to perceive a high risk for all banks.

The likelihood function $L(n \mid \theta_i)$ is the density function for the total number of bank failures, i.e., the random variable $n_A + n_B$, given that θ equals θ_i. Using properties of the likelihood function assumed, we can derive the following conditions. Given $\theta_1 < \theta_2$,

$$L(n \mid \theta_1) > L(n \mid \theta_2) \qquad \text{if } n < n^*$$

$L(n \mid \theta_1) = L(n \mid \theta_2)$ if $n = n^*$

$L(n \mid \theta_1) < L(n \mid \theta_2)$ if $n > n^*$ **(C4)**

where $n^* = N \cdot (p_B - p_A) \cdot (\theta_2 - \theta_1)$ /

$$\ln[\{p_A + \theta_2 \cdot (p_B - p_A)\} / \{p_A + \theta_1 \cdot (p_B - p_A)\}]$$

(See Appendix 1)

E4 (the equation determining x_t) and C4 (the condition showing the magnitude of the likelihood functions) say that the estimate of x, i.e., the probability that the proportion of speculative banks is θ_1, decreases whenever the observed number of failures exceeds n^*, and vice versa. Algebraically,

$x_t < x_{t-1}$ if $n_{t-1} > n^*$

$x_t > x_{t-1}$ if $n_{t-1} < n^*$ **(C5)**

The critical number n^* lies between the expected number of failures given θ equals θ_1 and that given θ equals θ_2. Algebraically,

$E(n \mid \theta=\theta_1) < n^* < E(n \mid \theta=\theta_2)$ **(C6)**

(See Appendix II)

Note that n^* is constant over time since the likelihood functions remain the same due to constant p_A, p_B, and N.
In addition,

$\Delta\{L(n \mid \theta_1) / L(n \mid \theta_2)\} / \Delta n$ **(C7)**

(See Appendix III)

In words, the ratio of $L(n \mid \theta_1)$ to $L(n \mid \theta_2)$ monotonically decreases as n increases. Applying this condition to E4, x_t monotonically decreases as n_{t-1} increases, for a given x_{t-1}.

Combining the results of this section, we can describe the effect of a large number of bank failures on the expected return from deposits as follows. When a large number of bank failures is observed, it is more likely that the proportion of speculative banks is high. Thus, depositors perceive a high probability of their own banks being speculative. This depositors' perception results in a high estimated probability of failure, which applies to all banks. Thus, the expected return from deposits becomes low. Hence, the observation of a large number of bank failures produces a low expected return from deposits. This result stems from the lack of bank specific information. If such information were available, depositors would not infer the soundness of individual banks from the condition of the banking system as a whole.

1.f. Bank Runs

Bank runs occur when the asset that is optimal for individuals shifts from deposits to self-storage, i.e., when the expected return from deposits becomes lower than the return from self-storage.

Combining C1 and E2, we can derive the condition that individuals hold deposit with respect to θ_t:

$$\theta_t < \{b \cdot (1 - q) \cdot (1 - p_A) - p_A \cdot B_1\} /$$

$$[\{b \cdot (1 - q) + B_1\} \cdot (p_B - p_A)] = \theta^* \qquad \text{(C8)}$$

By A8, $\theta_1 < \theta^* < \theta_2$.

In this economy, θ_t has to be estimated. θ_t is the mean value of the posterior distribution of θ. Thus, θ_t is determined by x_t, which summarizes the posterior distribution of θ. Combining E3 (the equation determining θ_t) and C8, the necessary condition for individuals to hold deposits is:

$$x_t > (\theta_2 - \theta^*) / (\theta_2 - \theta_1) = x^*$$

In turn, x_t critically depends on the number of failures in the previous period and on x_{t-1} which characterizes the prior distribution of θ.

   To illustrate how a bank run would occur, let's start from a situation in which everybody holds deposits, and the prior belief is that:

$$P(\theta = \theta_1) = 1 - \varepsilon = x_t > x^*$$

$$P(\theta = \theta_2) = \varepsilon = 1 - x_t$$

where ε is a very small number.

The return from deposits is lower than the return from self-storage if $x_t < x^*$.

   Given how individuals rationally infer θ, the probability of occurrence of bank runs depends on the true value of θ. By C6, $E(n \mid \theta = \theta_1) < n^* < E(n \mid \theta = \theta_2)$. Hence, when the true value of θ is θ_1, the average number of bank failures is smaller than n^*. A number of bank failures smaller than n^* results in an increase in x_t which is the estimate of x at time t (by C5) and hence a decrease in θ_t (by E3). Accordingly, x_t converges to 1, and θ_t converges to θ_1. By the same analogy, the true θ value of θ_2 produces an upward movement of the estimate of θ until it reaches θ_2. Hence, θ_t approaches the true value of θ over time. This result rests on a nature of the Bayesian inference; the estimated distribution approaches the true distribution as the sample size increases.

   Suppose the true value of θ is θ_1. A low value of θ does not completely eliminate the possibility of bank runs since the number of bank failures is stochastic. However, the probability is very low; usually, one sample does not significantly alter the prior belief. C5 indicates that x_t tends to increase over time when θ is θ_1. Occasionally, the number of failures will be large due to the stochastic nature of withdrawals, but this may not be enough to cause x_t to fall below x^*.

Now suppose that the true value of θ is θ_2. Then it is highly likely that depositors observe large numbers of failures in succession, which would make x_t decrease over time (By C5). If x_t decreases until it falls below x^*, depositors estimate θ to be larger than θ^*. Then the optimal asset for depositors becomes self-storage instead of deposits. Hence, there will be a run on all banks.

In this model, bank runs are a consequence of the inability of individuals to distinguish between type A and type B banks. Since they are treated equally by depositors, conservative banks end up sharing the problems of speculative ones that have weaker financial structure.

2. GOVERNMENT PROVISION OF INSURANCE

In a system with government provision of deposit insurance, depositors are not concerned about the risk of individual banks. Financial strength may differ across banks. However, banks are perceived by depositors to be identical in terms of deposit risks since deposits are covered by reliable government insurance. Given this perception, security is not a factor in attracting depositors. Thus, banks have no incentive to prove their creditworthiness to depositors. Moreover, a risk-insensitive premium structure, which is a property of the government insurance of the U.S., does not encourage banks to demonstrate their relative strength to the insurance agency either. Naturally, banks would not make the costly effort of providing information about their financial strength. As a result, bank-specific information is missing.

Lacking the information, in our model, the public infers the soundness of individual banks from the condition of the entire banking system, which is measured by the bank failure ratio. Hence, in analyzing the behavior of the public, most properties of the previous model are preserved. A large number of bank failures continue to signal an adverse condition of the banking sector and a high probability of failures of individual banks.

Government deposit insurance may affect the profit maximizing behavior of banks since it takes away incentives to monitor banks from the public. Hence, if the government does not regulate banks, there will be serious moral hazard problems which may increase the probability of bank failures. The provision of insurance without regulation would not produce a viable system. With regulation by the government, the question is the effectiveness of monitoring by different agents; which agent is more effective in preventing banks from taking excessive risks, the government or the public? The answer may depend on the tightness of the government regulation. But then the matter becomes further complicated by the welfare costs associated with banking regulation. The effect of government insurance on the probability of bank failures is undoubtedly an important banking issue and also pertinent to this study in that a change in the probability affects the possibility of bank failure contagion. However, as suggested above, the combined effects of government insurance and regulation on the probability of bank failures are ambiguous. Due to this ambiguity, it is not possible in the present context to generalize their roles in the contagion of bank failures. Thus, this model does not attempt to endogenize the risk taking behavior of banks and resulting changes in the probability of bank failures.

For the purpose of studying the contagion issue, the major modification to the previous model necessitated by the incorporation of insurance is the estimation of the expected return from deposits. Deposit insurance lessens public anxiety about the soundness of individual banks. Upon observing a large number of bank failures, depositors may perceive that banks are unsound. Nevertheless, depositors will not estimate a high probability of deposit losses as long as they believe that the insurance mechanism will remain sound. The insurance acts as a buffer, which absorbs shocks occurring in the banking sector. However, when the likelihood of the banking system being sound is very low, the reliability of the insurance mechanism itself starts eroding.[7] In other words, a sufficiently large shock can still be damaging even if it is partially cushioned by the buffer. In order to completely prevent runs on banks, the government needs to commit a gigantic amount of resources to the insurance. Thus, the government provision of deposit insurance also involves high social costs.

In algebraic terms, E1 is restated as:

$$E_t(C) = (e_t - \alpha) \cdot (1 - B_1) + \{1 - (e_t - \alpha)\} \cdot q$$

$$+ \{1 - (e_t - \alpha)\} \cdot (1-q) \cdot (1+b) \qquad \text{for } e_t > \alpha$$

$$E_t(C) \approx q + (1 - q) \cdot (1 + b) \qquad \text{for } e_t < \alpha$$

Deposit insurance creates a gap between the probability of bank failures and the probability of deposit losses. α captures the security provided by insurance. The probability of deposit losses is:

$$e_t - \alpha = (1-\theta_t) \cdot p_A + \theta_t \cdot p_B - \alpha \qquad \text{for } e_t > \alpha$$

$$\approx 0 \qquad \text{for } e_t < \alpha$$

As is in the basic model, a high bank failure ratio signals that the condition of the banking sector is weak and hence the probability of bank failures is high. Accordingly, e_t is estimated in the same manner. However, as long as the insurance agency remains capable of paying off depositors, the high failure ratio does not signal the risk that depositors may not be repaid. Thus, the expected return from deposits can still be high enough to make deposits attractive even when the proportion of speculative banks is high. Depositors discount the risk by α.

The condition of bank runs can be obtained by combining these results with C8. Bank runs occur when:

$$\theta_t > \theta^I = \{b \cdot (1 - q) \cdot (1 - p_A + \alpha) - (p_A - \alpha) \cdot B_1\} /$$

$$[\{b \cdot (1 - q) + B_1\} \cdot (p_B - p_A)]$$

$$> \{b \cdot (1 - q) \cdot (1 - p_A) - p_A \cdot B_1\} /$$

$$[\{b \cdot (1 - q) + B_1\} \cdot (p_B - p_A)] = \theta^*$$

Given $\theta^I > \theta^*$, the critical level of x_t is lower. Hence, in the presence of insurance, it takes a larger number of failures to alarm the public and to start bank runs.

θ^I is an increasing function of α, which in turn is an increasing function of the reliability of the insurance mechanism. Backed up by the Treasury,[8] government insurance is certainly more reliable than privately provided insurance or any other private efforts to prevent bank runs. Therefore, government deposit insurance effectively fortifies the banking sector. The required resources to completely eliminate the possibility of bank runs, however, can be extremely large.

3. BANKING SYSTEM
WITHOUT GOVERNMENT INTERVENTION

This section explores a world of no government intervention and analyzes the vulnerability of the banking system to runs. The system is assumed to be deregulated, and the government does not provide insurance. The crucial feature of this deregulated system is that depositors are concerned about the safety of individual banks. The cost of bank failures can no longer be transferred to the government.

Let's dwell on the same banking structure delineated in the basic model; the proportion of speculative banks is θ. In this competitive world, depositors consider both the rate of return offered and safety in selecting their banks. Hence, speculative and conservative banks can coexist. Speculative banks survive by offering a high rate of return, and conservative ones attract depositors by proving their financial strength, i.e., by providing information.

Given that banks have incentives to misrepresent their type, it would be costly for depositors to process information. Thus, mere disclosure would not constitute reliable information provision. Banks will have to bear information processing costs. Banks may hire an outside auditor who is concerned about his/her own reputation, or they may restrict themselves by making precommitments, similar to bond covenants, to depositors. Alternatively, banks belonging to a similar risk class may form a coalition such that the membership signals the riskiness of member banks. Then banks having a superior information processing ability watch each other and eliminate banks with worse risks in order to maintain the reputation of the group.

When banks provide financial information, depositors have a prior notion of the type of their banks. For the purpose of analyzing the contagion effect running from speculative banks to conservative ones, it is sufficient to look at the behavior of individuals having deposits with the banks that are deemed to be conservative. A depositor belonging to this group has some information specific to his bank in addition to an estimate of θ.

It is natural for depositors to rely primarily on bank specific information when it is available. However, if this information is less than perfect, the failure ratio may remain as a relevant variable supplementing the primary information. A high estimate of θ due to a high failure ratio can be an indication that some supposedly conservative banks have switched their financial policies, or that the asset position of some previously sound banks has been impaired by failures of other banks or by an exogenous shock. Thus, suspicion arises when θ seems high; it can be my bank whose financial position has changed. Algebraically, they estimate the probability of bank failures:

$$e_t = (1 - \mu \cdot \theta_t) \, p_A + \mu \cdot \theta_t \cdot p_B$$

$$= p_A + \mu \cdot \theta_t \cdot (p_B - p_A) \qquad 0 \leq \mu \leq 1 \tag{E5}$$

When the information possessed by depositors indicates the soundness of a bank, the probability of the bank being unsound is lower than the economywide proportion of speculative banks. μ captures the quality of information possessed by individuals.

$\mu = 1$, no information.
In this case, E5 is the same as E2 of the basic model.

$\mu = 0$, perfect information.
Depositors are sure that their banks are sound.

Given this specification, bank runs occur when:

$$\theta_t > \theta^F = \{ b \cdot (1 - q) \cdot (1 - p_A) - p_A \cdot B_1 \} \, /$$

$$[\{ b \cdot (1 - q) + B_1 \} \cdot (p_B - p_A) \cdot \mu]$$

$$> \{ b \cdot (1 - q) \cdot (1 - p_A) - p_A \cdot B_1 \} \, /$$

$$[\{ b \cdot (1 - q) + B_1 \} \cdot (p_B - p_A)] = \theta^*$$

θ^F increases as μ decreases. Thus, bank runs are less contagious when depositors are better informed. The availability of bank-specific information reduces the signalling effect of individual bank failures. Therefore, a banking system without government insurance may not be so vulnerable to runs. Sound banks can prevent runs on themselves if they are able to provide reliable information about their financial structure.

4. SUMMING-UP

This chapter has recognized incomplete information as the major source of bank failure contagion. In the basic model, depositors lacking bank-specific information infer the soundness of the banks of their concern from the condition of the banking system as a whole. Hence, when an adverse condition of the banking sector is signalled by a high bank failure ratio, depositors run on banks in general. In this situation, speculative behavior of a subset of banks causes problems for all banks by making bank failures contagious.

Government deposit insurance lowers the probability of deposit losses and hence prevent banks runs. However, little bank-specific information is available when the government provides deposit insurance. It can be very costly to prevent depositors lacking bank-specific information from running on banks.

When the government does not intervene and refuses to bear the cost of bank failures, banks have very strong incentives to provide financial information. Hence, if banks find ways to provide their financial information in a reliable manner, it is possible that the provision of information supersedes the provision of insurance by the government. Given this possibility, bank runs do not imply inherent instability of competitive banking.

NOTES

1. Bank panics result in an excessive liquidity premium on currency and hence substantially lower prices of other assets in terms of currency. Then previously sound banks may become insolvent when a panic occurs. I exclude this possibility in defining what is to be meant here by a "sound" bank.
2. A stands for assumption, C for condition, and E for equation.
3. A net return of zero has been chosen for analytical convenience. A selection of any amount between $\{1-(b/q-b)\}$ and $1+b$ would not affect any qualitative results of this model. $\{1-(b/q-b)\}$ is the value at which the expected return from deposits equals that from self-storage assuming the probability of bank failure is zero. Thus a return to prematurely withdrawn deposits lower than $\{1-(b/q-b)\}$ will result in strict domination of self-storage over deposits. Obviously, a deposit contract offering a higher return to prematurely withdrawn deposits than to matured deposits is not viable. Besides these restrictions, analyses of this model do not depend on the return to prematurely withdrawn deposits.
4. In the event of a bank failure, some type 1 depositors may withdraw before the bank fails and receive 1 unit. This possibility is deliberately omitted to simplify algebraic manipulations. The essential feature of this model is that $E(C)$ is a decreasing function of e. This property will still be preserved when some depositors of a failed bank receive 1 unit.
5. An implicit assumption is that solvent banks are more liquid as well.
6. We will see later that this simplifying assumption makes no difference to our qualitative results.
7. Major failures can easily exhaust the insurance fund. For example, the pay-off to depositors of two Orange County (California) S & L institutions that failed on June 6, 1988, American Diversified Savings Bank and North America Savings and Loan, amounted to $1.35 billion, which was almost half of FSLIC's $3 billion nationwide fund. The exhaustion of the FSLIC fund and political uncertainties led to deposit drains from S & L institutions at the beginning of 1989.

8. The advantages enjoyed by the government insurance can be found in Federal Deposit Insurance Act of 1950. Sec.14 of the act states, "The Corporation(FDIC) is authorized to borrow from the Treasury, and the Secretary of the Treasury is authorized and directed to loan to the Corporation at such terms as may be fixed by the Corporation and the Secretary, such funds as in the judgement of the Board of Directors of the Corporation are from time to time required for insurance purposes, not exceeding in aggregate $3,000,000,000 outstanding at any one time." In addition, Sec.15 states, "All notes, debentures,bonds or other such obligations issued by the Corporation shall be exempt, both as to principal and interest, from all taxation (except estate and inheritance taxes) now or hereafter imposed by the United States, by any Territory, dependency, or possession thereof, or any State, county, municipality, or local taxing authority."

CHAPTER IV

Bank Failure Contagion
in Historical Perspective

This chapter examines bank panics in U.S. history and the methods used to manage those panics. Historically, the United States had a more competitive banking structure than other countries and experienced recurrent bank panics. Hence, U.S. history offers the best environment for testing the empirical consistency of the theories developed by the model.

The model shows that bank failures are contagious when the public does not have bank specific information. Thus, a better informed public is less likely to panic. This empirical chapter attempts to capture the relationship between the availability of information and panic behavior of depositors.

A basic proposition of the model is that information about individual banks' financial structure is too costly for depositors to collect and process. Thus, depositors maximize utility without the information unless banks provide it as a part of efforts to maximize profit. In the controlled environment of the basic model, no information was available at all. This situation is the most vulnerable to bank runs. Apparently, no information is an extreme case. Undoubtedly, the information problem has always existed. Yet the situation of no information does not approximate the real world either. It is a question of degree.

In U.S. history, the availability of information varied across panics. In some cases, more information was available by virtue of banks' efforts to provide financial information. In some others, depositors were able to obtain information for themselves at relatively low costs. Recognizing the varying availability of information, we should be able to find association between the availability of information and the magnitude of panic. When depositors were better informed, the contagion effect should be weaker, and *vice versa*. Empirical findings of such a relationship would constitute convincing evidence for the importance of information.

This chapter supports the relationship between bank-specific information and bank panics using two approaches. The association of a less dramatic panic with more information implies that a bank panic can be stopped mainly by means of information provision. The symptom should disappear if the cause for a disease is removed. Hence, as an approach to study the relationship, this chapter examines the ways in which financial crises were managed. The second approach compares different financial crises and shows the relationship between the magnitude of panic and the cost of information which can be measured by the degree of difficulty in understanding the cause of bank failures.

When a financial crisis came, the private sector and the government employed various devices to terminate the crisis. Those devices include bank suspension, issuance of clearing house loan certificates, and equalization of reserves. These measures not only enhance the liquidity of banks, but they also convey information.

Each method is of a different nature, and hence has different information content. The first section shows that a method with more information content performed better in stopping bank failure contagion. The section shows the effectiveness of a method with more information content by comparing clearing house loan certificates and equalization of reserves. The second section argues that the major role of bank suspension is the provision of solvency information rather than the enhancement of liquidity of banks. In other words, the effectiveness of bank suspension derives mainly from the information it provides. The analysis will focus on the bank reopening procedure following the nationwide bank suspension of 1933.

Depositors should be better informed if the cost of information is low. An informed public would not run on solvent banks. Bank failures may result in the insolvency of some banks that have a close financial connection with the failed banks. Then an informed public would run on those insolvent banks, making bank failures somewhat contagious. However, the sound majority should not experience bank runs.[1] Thus, if the model is correct, bank runs should not spread widely when the information cost is low. The relevant information concerns the difference in the financial strength among banks. Depositors are said to be well informed if they can clearly perceive that banks in operation have stronger financial structure than that of previously failed banks; some banks failed due to a problem specific to those banks, and other banks do not have the same problem. The cost of information increases with the degree of difficulty involved in collecting and interpreting the information. Information cost is low when the general public, who are not endowed with sophisticated knowledge of banking in general and the condition of individual banks, can easily obtain and understand the information.

The model, which singles out incomplete information as the major source of contagion, predicts that a low information cost should be associated with a less dramatic panic. Hence, the third section compares bank panics in U.S. history and shows the association between the cost of information and the magnitude of panic. In examining different banking panics, particular attention will be paid to the financial crisis of 1884. The incident of 1884 is particularly interesting since the above mentioned relation was notably pronounced in the rather unique case.

1. CLEARING HOUSE LOAN CERTIFICATES AND EQUALIZATION OF RESERVES

Prior to the establishment of the Federal Reserve System (1913), the banking sector relied primarily on collective efforts to manage bank runs. Those efforts included the issuance of clearing house loan certificates and the practice of equalizing reserves.

These collective efforts were not all equally successful. Very commonly, the success has been attributed to the improved liquidity of banks; the goal of allaying financial panics was achieved by the provision of additional liquidity to banks.[2] This study interprets the role of such collective measures differently. Collective efforts could be successful because of information that they provided. Most of the collective efforts provided information as well as enhanced liquidity, and it was the provision of information that played the major role in tranquilizing bank panics.

1.a. Clearing House Loan Certificates

Clearing house loan certificates were the most frequently used device to manage bank runs before the establishment of the Federal Reserve System.[3] Empirically, the loan certificates were reasonably successful, especially in quieting minor panics. For example, in 1860 and 1861, they enabled banks to pass through periods of severe strain without suspension.[4] The loan certificates were highly regarded as effective by contemporary authors in allaying even major financial crises such as the panic of 1884.[5]

Clearing house loan certificates were an interbank settlement device. During a crisis, banks acquired the loan certificates by depositing qualifying assets with the Clearing House Association.[6] Then the loan certificates were used in lieu of legal reserves in making interbank settlements. This arrangement enabled banks to avoid costly liquidation of their assets. Thus, the loan certificates improved the liquidity position of banks when it was difficult to liquidate assets due to a financial crisis.

In addition to liquidity enhancement, clearing house loan certificates provided information that verified the asset position of banks. Banks acquiring the loan certificates were required to deposit securities with a committee appointed by the Clearing House Association. These securities would be easily marketable under normal financial circumstances. The following is the statements found on the clearing house loan certificates issued in 1884:[7]

> This certifies that the ____ National bank has deposited with the committee securities in accordance with the proceedings of a meeting of the association held May 14, 1884, upon which this certificate is issued. This certificate will be received in payment of balances at the clearing-house for the sum of ten thousand dollars from any member of the Clearing-House Association. On the surrender of the certificate by the depositing bank above named, the committee will endorse the amount as a payment on the obligation of said bank, held by them, and surrender a proportionate share of collateral securities held therefor.

Furthermore, it was a policy of the Clearing House, which was an organization consisting of profit-maximizing banks, to issue the certificates to a member bank when the association was convinced of not only the quality of the assets deposited but also the overall asset position of the bank. Given this nature, the loan certificates certified that the holder of the certificates was experiencing not a solvency problem but merely a liquidity problem. Hence, it conveyed information about the soundness of a bank; insolvent banks were not allowed to obtain the loan certificates, so the banks having the loan certificates were fundamentally solvent.

Theoretically, it is very difficult, if not impossible, to judge whether the enhancement of liquidity or the provision of information was the more important factor. Hence, it is more sensible to employ an empirical approach and compare clearing house loan certificates with equalization of reserves. The two measures are similar in improving the liquidity of banks. However, with regard to information provision, the two devices differ sharply. The analysis focuses on the theoretical distinctions between clearing house loan certificates and equalization of reserves and the empirical contribution of the two different measures in tranquilizing financial panics. This comparison will shed some light on the importance of the provision of information relative to the enhancement of liquidity.

1.b. Equalization of Reserves

Equalization of reserves was the practice of centrally pooling all legal reserves of member banks in an emergency and granting member banks equal access to the centralized reserve pool. When the New York Clearing House Association adopted equalization of reserves in 1873, the legal tender belonging to the associated banks became a common fund. A committee appointed by the association was authorized to manage the fund. The association required all member banks to participate fully in the plan and resolved to expel any member banks that declined to participate.[8] Banks generally made payments in checks that were certified as "good through the Clearing House."[9] Thus, the burden of paying legal tender was transferred to the Clearing House which was authorized to raise the necessary fund by assessing on banks with relatively large reserves. The management of the fund including the assessment was left at the discretion of the special committee.

Apparently, reserve pooling relieves the banks having insufficient reserves from difficulties of settling balances with other banks. Banks do not need to make physical deliveries of legal reserves among themselves. Interbank settlements can be made by accounting entries. In addition, equalization of reserves reduces stochastic withdrawal risks. When reserves are pooled, the standard deviation of withdrawals increases proportionately less than the amount of reserves. In other words, while some banks can suffer unexpectedly large withdrawals, others may experience less withdrawals than expected. Thus, the "bad luck" of some banks can be offset by the "good luck" of others. This effect reduces the vulnerability of the banking system to stochastic withdrawals.

Clearing house loan certificates and equalization of reserves both facilitate interbank settlements. With the reduced possibility of adverse clearing, banks would experience less pressure for liquidity in a panic. Then the necessary loan contraction might not be substantial. In this respect, clearing house loan certificates and equalization of reserves alleviate the liquidity problem of the banking system in a panic. However, neither of the two increases the total amount of reserves of the banking system as a whole, and hence fails to enlarge the system's capacity to make loans. This is undoubtedly true for equalization of reserves. The loan certificates increase the lending capacity of one bank at the expense of some other bank. Thus, there is no net effect. The loan certificates do not constitute a legal reserve for loan expansion purposes.[10] Suppose bank 1 settles a balance with bank 2 by "paying" the loan certificates. This settlement using loan certificates enables bank 1 to avoid a decrease in legal tender and to retain a larger lending capacity than it would otherwise. On the other hand, bank 2 loses an opportunity for loan expansion to which it is entitled. Instead, bank 2 is compensated for this foregone opportunity by interest payments on the loan certificates. Hence, the total lending capacity of the banking system as a whole is not affected either by reserve pooling or by the loan certificates. As mentioned above, equalization of reserves has an advantage over clearing house loan certificates, namely, the reduced stochastic withdrawal risks. Equalization of reserves better protects a bank from the withdrawals of currency that would not return to the banking system. Therefore, with regard to liquidity enhancement, the equalization of reserves should be at least as effective as issuance of clearing house loan certificates.

The main distinction rests on the information content of the two arrangements. During a banking crisis, banks can be classified into three groups: already failed banks (group A), banks suffering excessive withdrawals (group B), and those not experiencing difficulties yet (group C). The issuance of clearing house loan certificates to group B banks distinguishes group B banks from group A banks by conveying the message that group B banks have enough sound assets unlike group A banks. On the other hand, equalization of reserves does not convey any information about whether a particular bank belongs in group A or group B. Although the liquidity of group B banks can be enhanced by equalization of reserves, the soundness of assets held by group B banks is not verified by it. Hence, equalization of reserves fails to distinguish group B banks from group A banks in terms of their fundamental solvency. Instead, it erases the distinction among group B and group C banks by allowing all of them to have the equal access to the centralized reserves. Hence, equalization of reserves not only fails to provide additional information but also obscures existing information. In sum, while clearing house loan certificates provide information about banks' solvency, equalization of reserves fails to distinguish solvent banks from insolvent ones.

1.c. The Panic of 1873

Since the organization of the National Banking System, equalization of reserves was practiced only once in the U.S., namely, in 1873.[11] The episode of 1873 well illustrates the importance of the provision of information. For the purpose of providing background knowledge, this section briefly describes the developments surrounding the panic and the equalization of reserves.

The most notable phenomenon preceding the panic of 1873 was the expansion of loans mainly to railroad companies. As a result, the money market was overloaded with debts (high debt-equity ratios of business firms and banks), and speculation at the New York Stock Exchange was much more active than usual.[12] The situation, hence, was very vulnerable to a financial crisis. The *Bankers' Magazine* describes the condition of the financial market in August, 1873 as follows:[13]

> The money market has become quite easy during the month of August, with a minimum rate this week of 4 per cent. on call loans. Commercial paper is not abundant and is readily taken by bankers and brokers at six to seven per cent. The demand for money in New York, arises mainly on account of new railroad enterprises throughout the country. The present construction of new railroads for the year 1873 will cover over six thousand miles, which at thirty thousand dollars per mile, will consume about one hundred and eighty millions of capital - one-half in money and the remainder in bonds.[14]

The crisis came in September. Failures of major financial institutions startled the market; Warehouse Security company failed on Sep. 8, and Kenyon, Cox and Co. on Sep. 13 due to heavy advances made to railroad companies. These failures were followed by numerous other financial institutions, mostly those engaged in the negotiation of railroad loans. These events precipitated a panic in stocks and bank deposits. The number of failures peaked on September 20 (Saturday). The list of suspensions and failures on that day included Union Trust Co., National Trust Co., Union Banking Co., and National Bank of the Common Wealth.

On September 20, New York Clearing House Association called an emergency meeting and adopted two major plans, namely, the authorization of $10,000,000 in clearing house loan certificates and the equalization of reserves. This decision was made in the morning. On the same day, the New York Stock Exchange was closed at noon.[15] The *Nation* depicts the stock market's reaction to the attempts made by the Clearing House:[16]

> Unfortunately, this was an evidence of their depletion gratifying to the bears. Prices were receding still lower; the difficulty of getting checks certified, however, and the distrust of the condition of the banks, made dealings hazardous to all but those who had provided a store of bank bills for this occasion. The sellers of stock prayed for a cessation of dealings, and at noon on Saturday the exchange was closed, and so remained at the date of our going to press.

This event illustrates the importance of information in stopping panics.

In the following week, depositors ceased running upon the particular banks targeted previously. However, they started withdrawing deposits from banks in general.[17] During the week, only one bank in New York city was suspended.[18] In contrast, the system as a whole showed signs of suffering. At the end of the week, Friday, September 26, the bank statement showed that New York banks had specie of $12,937,300 and deposits of $174,527,800, representing decreases, from one week earlier, of $5,907,500 and $23,512,300 respectively. In percentage terms, specie and deposits held by banks decreased by 31.3 percent and 11.9 percent.[19] As a result, the average percentage of reserves held by the New York city banks dropped to 16.97 percent from 23.23 percent of the previous week, recording a decrease of 6.96 percent. In terms of bank failures, previous two weeks, the weeks spanning from September 7 to September 20, were much more chaotic. However, the percentage of reserves decreased by only about 1 percentage point per week; the figures were 24.95 percent on September 6 and 23.89 percent on September 13. Table 2 summarizes the financial condition of New York banks during the month of September.

The Clearing House Association found that the system could not sustain withdrawals any longer. Realizing the necessity of further actions, it authorized an additional issue of clearing house loan certificates in the amount of $10,000,000 on September 24, doubling the total amount. Subsequently, this restriction on the total amount had to be removed since the whole amount was used up during the following two days.[20] At the same time, the Treasury suspended the Bank Act and thereby the 25% reserve requirement on national banks, and became more active in purchasing government bonds. More importantly, New York banks suspended currency payments on September 24. Shortly, the suspension extended to other large cities, making the panic nationwide and economywide.[21] During the suspension, banks paid nothing but small checks in legal tender, and large calls were met by the "certification" of checks whose redemption in legal tender was deferred until the termination of the crisis.[22]

The financial unrest continued in October.[23] The Comptroller of the Currency reported that the banks of the city of New York held the smallest amount of legal tender notes on October 13, during the crisis.[24] Meanwhile, the liquidations of insolvent financial institutions were undertaken by banking authorities, and most of them were completed in October. Finally, the system started showing signs of recovery toward the end of October.

On October 24, the Clearing House banks passed a resolution that the "pooling" arrangement be discontinued on and after November 1. However, they decided to continue for mutual safety the use of the loan certificates.[25] New York banks also resumed currency payments on the first day of November, the same day on which they dissolved the bank pool of legal tender.

Although the financial condition was improving toward the end of October, it was far from having fully recovered. Furthermore, a very unfavorable event occurred on October 30 when the failure of Hayt, Sprague & Co. was announced. The huge company, engaged in multiple enterprises such as milling, printing, railroads, steamboat, iron foundries, and locomotive works, had significant influence on the economy. The failure renewed the distrust in the financial market. Hence, there were uncertainties about the recovery of the financial market after the resumption of currency payments and the dissolution of the bank pool of reserves. Nevertheless, the financial market showed steady recovery during the month of November.[26] Table 3 shows the financial condition of banks of New York City during the months of October and November. Taking Oct. 13 as the lowest point, we can unambiguously conclude from the table that the recovery in November was much more notable than that in October. The recovery was especially pronounced in the deposit figures which might best reflect public confidence in the banking system. Given these developments, it appears that equalization of reserves failed to make any positive contribution to restoring public confidence. The attempt to stop bank runs by equalizing reserves was a complete failure.

1.d. Interpretation and Conclusion.

The experience of 1873 may be interpreted in the following way. The equalization of reserves implemented in 1873 partially restored public confidence in problem banks but did so at the expense of the whole banking system, thus aggravating the situation. Equalization of reserves may be viewed as problem sharing.[27] Depositors knew that some banks had problems. When they learned that banks shared the problems by pooling reserves, depositors conjectured that the entire banking system might become fragile. Public confidence in the banking system as a whole was eroded by this practice.

This episode tells us the importance of information provision relative to liquidity enhancement. Undoubtedly, the dominant function of the equalization of reserves is to supply liquidity to problem banks. With regard to the provision of information, the contribution of reserve pooling is negative. The relevant information is the distinction among banks in terms of financial strength. For depositors with some notion of the distinction, it becomes vaguer when reserves are pooled. Depositors have one less factor, namely, the level of reserves, to use for the assessment of banks' financial positions. On the other hand, clearing house loan certificates allow banks to demonstrate their asset positions. The relative success of clearing house loan certificates rests on this difference. Hence, the effectiveness of clearing house loan certificates is attributable to the information they provide. The moral of this episode is that we need to provide information to effectively subdue financial crises.

This section has shown the important role of the information about the solvency of banks in tranquilizing financial crises. From this episode, we can also infer that depositors' major concern is not the liquidity but the solvency of banks, which is more fundamental. Real problems arise when the public becomes suspicious about the solvency of banks. This suspicion can hardly be erased by tentative improvement of liquidity. The enhancement of liquidity may delay the failure of an insolvent bank, but it is only a matter of time before the insolvent bank fails. What is needed to restore public confidence is the information that banks have sufficient assets to meet all of their liabilities. Fundamentally sound banks can avoid the contagion of bank runs by proving their solvency to the public.

2. SUSPENSION OF BANKS AND THE CRISIS OF 1933

Financial crises often led to suspensions of payments by banks implemented on a regional or national level. One major aspect of financial crises is massive withdrawals of bank deposits. Individual banks were forced to close their doors when depositors demanded abnormally large withdrawals. Banks also collectively suspended payments in the last resort to end widespread bank runs.

When banks reopened their doors after suspension, runs on those banks did not recur in most cases.[28] The most common belief is that the main purpose of suspension was to provide banks with the time to improve their liquidity positions.[29] Accordingly, it was the enhanced liquidity that enabled banks to survive.[30] This section interprets bank suspension differently. The emphasis will be given to the other aspect of bank suspension, namely, the provision of information.

Bank suspension was always followed by a thorough examination conducted by banking authorities.[31] Depending on the examination results, problem banks were placed in the hands of receivers for liquidation, and others were permitted to reopen after their solvency was confirmed. It appears that the elimination of insolvent banks during suspension and the assured solvency of reopened banks were of more significance than supplying liquidity. Bank suspension provided an opportunity to weed out problem banks, while minimizing perturbation in the market that might be caused by the closure of insolvent banks. This point is supported by policies pursued by the Comptroller of the Currency during suspension. In its Annual Report of 1893, the Comptroller recognized depositors' suspicion of the solvency of banking institutions as the main cause for a large number of suspensions, and stated its policy:[32]

> With a full knowledge of the general solvency of these institutions and the cause which brought about their suspension, the policy was inaugurated of giving all banks, which, under ordinary circumstances would not have closed, and whose management had been honest, an opportunity to resume business. This policy was one which seemed to commend itself to the Comptroller as proper to pursue under the

circumstances, and it is believed that the result have justified the experiment of its adoption.

In no instance has any bank been permitted to resume on money borrowed or for which as an association it has become liable. Whenever those active in the management of the banks resuming, either as executive officers or directors, have been debtors to such banks, their indebtness has been paid or secured, and whenever impairment of capital stock has been found, such impairment has been made good, either by voluntary or enforced assessment on the shareholders.

Granted this policy of the banking authorities, the public could understand that the banks allowed to reopen were solvent ones. Consequently, depositors felt safe and stopped withdrawing deposits.

This aspect of providing information was especially pronounced in the reopening procedure after the nationwide bank suspension of 1933. This section looks at the episode of 1933 in detail to confirm the importance of the provision of information.

2.a. Background

After the stock market crash of October 1929, a series of bank failures ensued. Between the end of December 1929 and the end of February 1933, nearly 5,500 banks, more than 20 percent of banks in the nation, suspended operation.[33] The bank failures seriously undermined public confidence and hence aggravated the situation. In 1932 alone, 1,456 banks were suspended out of a total of 19,163 banks.[34]

The devastating financial situation led to statewide bank suspensions. On October 31, 1932, a twelve day bank and business holiday was declared in Nevada. On February 4, 1933, the state of Louisiana declared a public holiday that was intended to provide respite for troubled banks. Michigan, which was a significantly larger economy, entered into an eight-day bank holiday on February 14, 1933.

The bank moratorium promulgated in Michigan inflamed bank runs everywhere in the nation. This financial panic troubled large banks with solid financial structure as well as problem banks. Even the soundest bank could not sustain simultaneously occurring difficulties such as withdrawals by other banks, those by local depositors, and international gold outflows.[35] During the first three days of March, withdrawals were proceeding at the weekly rate of almost 10 percent of total deposits.[36] The critical situation is described by a report of the Federal Reserve Board:[37]

> Between the early part of February and March 4, money in circulation increased by $1,830,000,000, of which $1,430,000,000 was in Federal Reserve notes and $320,000,000 in gold and gold certificates, and at the same time $300,000,000 of gold was withdrawn through earmarking. Nearly two thirds of these demands were concentrated in the week ending March 4. In order to obtain currency and gold, member banks, between early February and March 4, increased their bills discounted at the Federal Reserve banks by over $1,160,000,000 and drew down their reserve balances by over $500,000,000. At the same time the Reserve banks increased their holdings of purchased bills by $390,000,000 and of United States Government securities by nearly $100,000,000.

This bank panic compelled most other states to suspend or limit the banking business.

2.b. Proclamation of the National Bank Holiday

Franklin D. Roosevelt was inaugurated as president of the United States on March 4, inheriting the tremendous burden of ending the banking panic and of making the economic strength of the nation recover. At the time of the inauguration, it seemed highly unlikely that the banking system would survive the severe strain without major government intervention. Due to the imminent need, discussion of banking matters immediately followed the inauguration ceremony. Emergency action was called for. To prevent further withdrawals while preparing emergency banking legislation, Roosevelt proclaimed a national bank holiday on March 6 under the authority vested by the Trading with the Enemy Act of 1917, whose legal validity was dubious.[38]

The proclamation ordered that all banking institutions located in the United States of America, including the territories and insular possessions, suspend all banking transactions from Monday, March 6, to Thursday, March 9. The definition of banking institutions was very comprehensive, ranging from the Federal Reserve banks to any persons engaged in any form of banking business. The proclamation emphasized the prohibition of transactions that might facilitate currency hoarding or gold outflows, and specified a maximum penalty of $10,000 fine, or ten years' imprisonment, or both for willful violation. The Secretary of the Treasury, who was authorized to make exceptions to the proclamation, issued a series of measures that permitted some transactions involving economic necessities such as the distribution of food and medicine. Yet almost all major banking transactions remained prohibited during the suspension.

2.c. Reopening

The day before the declaration of the national bank holiday, March 5, Roosevelt summoned Congress to convene in extraordinary session on March 9, with a plan to have an emergency banking bill ready by that day. Thus, the administration had only a few days to draft emergency resolutions that should restore the strength of the banking system.

In order to thoroughly examine potential schemes within a short time, a committee was formed, comprised of bankers, banking authorities, congressional leaders, and members of the Hoover administration as well as members of the Roosevelt administration.

Owing to the severity of the condition, the prevailing opinion was that radical measures were imperative.[39]

The government guarantee of bank deposits was the most dominant opinion and hence became the first proposal. On March 6, a subcommittee, which was chaired by Davison of the Central Hanover Bank of New York, recommended a government deposit guarantee of 100 percent, 75 percent, 50 percent, and 25 percent depending on the condition of banks.[40] This proposal was opposed by the Administration which was inclined to minimal government intervention. Another proposal of significance was the immediate conversion of all government bonds into cash at par.[41] Again, the proposal was rejected for fear of inflation and reluctance to abandon the gold standard.

It was a dilemma to find a moderate solution to a financial crisis of unprecedented severity. Ogden Mills, secretary of the Treasury of the Hoover Administration, and George Harrison, governor of the Federal Reserve Bank of New York, finally came up with acceptable solutions.

Mills argued that not all banks should reopen immediately, and suggested that banks be reopened gradually, starting from the ones with the soundest financial structure. Mills proposal divided banks into three categories: (1) Class A banks - those of complete solvency and adequate liquidity, capable of immediate reopening if not hindered by fears of the collapse of weaker institutions; (2) Class B banks - banks whose capital structures based on present values were impaired, or were insolvent, or not liquid, or any combination of these, but capable of reorganization; and (3) Class C banks - banks so hopelessly insolvent that they should not be permitted to reopen at all.[42] According to this classification, class A banks should be allowed to resume business as soon as possible, class B banks after reorganization, while class C banks must be closed permanently.

Harrison proposed a scheme for providing liquidity, while retaining control over inflation. The plan was to authorize the

Federal Reserve banks to make short-term loans against sound bank assets.[43]

The Emergency Banking act of 1933 was drafted on the basis of these proposals. Recognizing the emergency, Congress approved the bill on March 9 with little dispute. The act authorized the President of the United States to regulate the banking business in an emergency, and the Federal Reserve banks to issue circulating notes.[44] These measures became the legal basis for the bank reopening under a licensing system.

Using the authority granted by the act, Roosevelt issued a proclamation on March 9, which extended the bank holiday until further proclamation. On the following day, March 10, the Secretary of the Treasury was authorized by executive order to permit banks to resume business. Bank reopenings started on March 13 and proceeded gradually. Sound banks in the twelve Federal Reserve cities reopened on March 13. On Tuesday, March 14, banks that were judged to be sound opened in about 250 cities having recognized clearing houses.[45] On succeeding days, banks in the smaller communities opened.

Withdrawals for the purpose of currency hoarding did not recur when banks were reopened. In fact, depositors not only stopped withdrawing but also started redepositing money in banks. The *Federal Reserve Bulletin* reports the recovery during the month following the suspension as follows:[46]

A rapid return flow of currency to the Reserve Banks has characterized the period since the reopening of licensed banks under the program announced by the president on March 10. Between March 4 and April 5, $1,225,000,000 of money returned to the Reserve Banks, of which $645,000,000 consisted of gold coin and gold certificate; the ratio of reserves against Federal Reserve notes and deposits combined advanced from 45.1 to 59.7 percent. Currency brought to the reserve banks by the member banks represented in part a return by these banks of cash previously withdrawn for the purpose of increasing their vault holdings and in part currency redeposited with the banks by the Public. Funds arising out of this return flow of currency were used by the member banks to reduce their borrowings at the reserve banks by $1,000,000,000, and in addition to reduce acceptance holdings of the reserve banks by $130,000,000.

Total reserves of the 12 Federal reserve banks combined advanced from $2,800,000,000 on March 4 to $3,490,000,000 on April 5, the highest level since the autumn of 1931. On April 7 the discount rate of the Federal Reserve Bank of New York was reduced from 3.5 to 3 percent.

The recovery continued. By the middle of April, deposits at the weekly reporting Federal Reserve member banks had increased by about $1.000,000,000, and the increase reached $2,000,000,000 before the end of June.[47]

Undoubtedly, the nationwide moratorium turned the banking situation around. The suspension was remarkable success by any standard. The question is what mechanism restored public confidence in such a short time. Mere suspension of banks would not help restore public confidence in any way unless accompanied by remedies for the banking problems. In search of such mechanisms, the next few sections will explore the important measures that accompanied the bank reopening.

2.d. The License System

With the broadened authority granted by the Emergency Banking Act, the Roosevelt administration established a licensing system for bank reopening. Under the system, only licensed banks were allowed to resume business. A presidential executive order regarding licensing of banks was issued on March 10. By the executive order, the Secretary of the Treasury was authorized to license any member banks of the Federal Reserve System and any other banking institutions organized under federal law to perform any or all of their usual banking functions. With regard to non-member state banking institutions, similar authority was conferred upon state banking authorities. In addition, the executive order designated the Federal Reserve banks as agents of the Secretary of the Treasury for receiving applications for the license and for the issuance of licenses upon approval of the Secretary.

The main function of the Federal Reserve banks was to evaluate and classify member banks according to their relative soundness. Upon receiving the applications for reopening, district Reserve banks examined the financial strength of state member banks, and recommended licensing to the Secretary. The financial strength of national banks were reviewed by the Office of the Comptroller of the Currency. Jointly with the Office of the Comptroller, Federal Reserve banks made recommendations for the licensing of national banks on the basis of the Comptroller's examination results. The licensing policy of the Treasury was to permit the banks whose soundness had been endorsed by a district bank and/or the Comptroller to resume operation.[48] State banking authorities supervised the reopening of state non-member banks using similar licensing procedures.

Consequently, banking authorities shared the examination duties in such a way that they could fully utilize the informational advantages possessed by each banking agent. Apparently, it was the Comptroller of the Currency that was most familiar with the financial data of national banks. While the district Federal Reserve banks were familiar with the financial conditions of state member banks, state banking authorities were best informed of the financial conditions of state non-member banks. In evaluating the financial conditions of banks, related agencies fully utilized available personnel which included officials and staff members of the Treasury, those of Federal Reserve banks, national bank examiners and field examiners.[49] Although the survey was performed within a short time, the evaluation results turned out to be fairly accurate thanks to the exhaustive efforts made by banking authorities and their informational advantages. Between the end of the bank holiday and the end of the year 1933, there were only 221 suspension cases among licensed banks, of which nine were national banks, six state member banks, and two hundred six non-member banks.[50] This statistic shows that only a few unsound banks were licensed.

The Emergency Banking Act empowered the Comptroller of the Currency to appoint a conservator who could be involved in the operation of a problem bank and direct the reorganization of the bank.[51] In addition, an executive order issued March 18 authorized state authorities to appoint a conservator for unlicensed state banks which were not under the control of the Comptroller. Grounded upon these legal provisions, the whole nation was able to pursue the reorganization and gradual reopening of unlicensed banks.

The Comptroller appointed conservators for banks whose financial structures were judged to be inadequate for immediate reopening but to have reorganization potential. Unlicensed banks with severely impaired financial structures were liquidated without the appointment of a conservator. The conservators' duties included the administration as well as the reorganization of unlicensed banks. While working on potential plans for reorganization, conservators assisted in providing essential banking services to the community by establishing separate trust funds consisting of new deposits. After reviewing the financial condition of the assigned bank in detail, each conservator determined the most appropriate reorganization plan for the bank or liquidated it if reorganization seemed impossible.

Reorganization plans adopted by conservators fell into three broad categories: capital correction plans, creditor waiver plans, and Spokane sale plans.[52] A capital correction plan was adopted if the market value of a bank's assets was greater than its liabilities. In these instances, the problem was an insufficient amount of capital. The impaired capital structure was corrected by stock holders' contributions or by issuance of preferred stocks.[53] Creditor waiver was utilized in those cases where the liabilities of a bank exceeded the appraised value of the assets, but not by a substantial percentage. The deficiency was eliminated by creditors' partial waiver of their claims, while the capital structure was restored by issuance of equity shares.[54] Under a Spokane sale plan, the conservator arranged a sound bank to take over the assets of an unlicensed bank at the fair market price and to continue banking business under a new name. Then the proceeds of sale were immediately distributed to the creditors of the old bank. A Spokane sale was not essentially different from liquidation, but it was preferred to ordinary liquidation when there existed community needs for the banking facilities. Out of 1,417 unlicensed national banks, 292 were reorganized under capital correction plans, 565 under creditor waiver plans, and 257 under Spokane sale plans. The rest, 303 banks, were liquidated.[55] The Comptroller of the Currency completed the reorganization of national banks on February 5, 1935 (See Table 4).

To recapitulate, the license to resume operation was issued only to those banks whose financial conditions were judged satisfactory. Unlicensed banks were permitted to reopen after their soundness was ensured by means of reorganization. Banking authorities liquidated those banks lacking the potential for reorganization. This verification of soundness characterized the procedure of licensing banks for reopening.

2.e. Liquidity Provision

Title IV of the Emergency Banking Act outlines the arrangements designed to rescue banks experiencing excessive withdrawals. It contains two major provisions facilitating liquidity supply to the financial market. One is designed to enhance the currency creating power of the Federal Reserve banks, and the other liberalizes the authority of the Federal Reserve banks to make loans to financial institutions.

Upon the deposit with the Treasurer of the United States of any direct obligations of the United States or of any notes, drafts, bills of exchange, or bankers' acceptance, the Federal Reserve banks were authorized to issue circulating notes. The maximum amount of the notes to be issued by the Federal Reserve banks were limited to the face value of the direct obligations of the United States and 90 percent of the estimated value of other securities. The circulating notes were subject to the same tax applied to the circulating notes of national banks.

This provision enlarged the capacity of the Federal Reserve banks to create currency by relaxing the collateral requirements. Initially, the security eligible for Federal Reserve notes was limited basically to gold or gold certificates. Government bonds could be used as the collateral, but on a very restricted basis.[56] For the purpose of easing the banking problem, the Glass-Steagall Act of 1932 relaxed the restrictions, upgrading direct obligations of the United States to a fully eligible collateral security. Other financial instruments were added to the list of the eligible securities by the Emergency Banking Act of 1933.

The Act authorized the Federal Reserve banks to make loans not only to member banks but also to other financial institutions. The Federal Reserve banks were empowered to make advances to member banks lacking eligible assets for rediscounting on its interest bearing notes secured by other sound assets of the banks. The interest had to be at least 1 percent per annum higher than the highest discount rate in effect. Recognizing that the banking problem was a national concern, Congress amended the Act on March 24, so that state non-member banks became eligible for the loans. State non-member banks were authorized to apply for advances to the Federal Reserve banks of their districts.[57] After they obtained such loans, non-member banks would be subjected to the same regulations applying to member banks. A similar authority to make loans to banks is found in the Glass-Steagall Act, but the act limited the scope of the banks eligible for the loans to member banks having a capital not exceeding $5,000,000. Thus, the significance of the Emergency Banking Act was to enlarge the scope to all banks.

Additional authority was conferred upon the Federal Reserve banks to make advances to any individual, partnership, or corporation on promissory notes secured by direct obligations of the United States. This additional power enabled the Federal Reserve banks to make loans to non-bank financial institutions. The terms of advances were limited to a maximum of 90 days, and the Federal Reserve banks retained the authority to determine and change the interest rate. Prior to the passage of the Emergency Banking Act, the Federal Reserve banks could discount papers of non-bank institutions arising out of actual commercial transactions, but not investment securities including government bonds.[58] In sum, the act provided a wide variety of financial institutions with relatively easy access to loans at the Federal Reserve banks.

Although more funds became available at Federal Reserve banks, the actual use of the fund was insignificant due to the remarkable recovery of public confidence. In fact, member banks reduced their borrowing at the Federal Reserve banks by about $1,000,000,000 during the first month following the resumption of operation.[59] The state of the new currency supply is nicely depicted by Lindley (1933):[60]

> In almost every city and town deposits exceeded withdrawals when the moratorium was lifted. The government had airplanes chartered to rush the new currency to the far corners of the country as rapidly as it came off the press. But they were not needed. Only a few thousand dollars' worth of the new Federal Reserve banknotes got into circulation.[61]

To recapitulate, the Emergency Banking Act facilitated the supply of liquidity by granting the Federal Reserve banks the power of creating more money and making loans on a more liberal basis. However, these measures were not required since few banks experienced excessive withdrawals after their reopening.

2.f. The First Presidential Fireside Chat

Being deeply concerned about the complicated banking situation, Roosevelt made a radio address on Sunday evening, March twelfth, 1933, which became the first of the famous fireside chat series.[62] Needless to say, the purpose was to lessen the anxiety and turmoil created by the nationwide bank suspension and the bank failures prior to the holiday. The address, which was an honest description of the banking situation and related future plans, helped greatly to restore public confidence in banking.

Roosevelt began the talk by explaining the mechanics of banking. He explained that even a very sound bank could experience difficulties when the withdrawal demand was abnormally large due to the loss of public confidence. This was because no bank was supposed to maintain the liquidity to meet all of its liabilities by keeping all the deposited money in its vault. Undeniably, the public had witnessed that almost all banks had been in trouble before the banking holiday was proclaimed. However, it did not mean that all banks were unsound. He emphasized that most of banks were in fact sound. What banks had faced was merely a liquidity problem.

Roosevelt continued the talk and described the reopening plan. By the Emergency Banking Act, he was authorized to extend the holiday and to develop a program to rehabilitate banks. Using the authority, he planned to permit only banks, "found to be all right" after careful examination, to reopen. The government did not want to have another epidemic of bank failures, and hence had a clear intention not to allow any problem banks to reopen without necessary rehabilitation.

Regarding the improvement of the liquidity of banks, Roosevelt called public attention to the fact that the Federal Reserve banks were allowed to issue additional currency on sound assets of banks. In addition, he emphasized the soundness of the additional currency to be issued, several times during the address: "It is sound currency because it is backed by actual, good assets."; "This currency is not fiat currency. It is issued only on adequate security - and every good bank has an abundance of such security."

He finished the talk by emphasizing that banks differed and hence should be differentiated, and assuring that the government would perform the job:

> We had a bad banking situation. Some of our bankers had shown
> themselves either incompetent or dishonest in their handlings of the
> people's funds. They had used the money entrusted to them in
> speculation and unwise loans. This was of course not true in the vast
> majority of our banks but it was true in enough of them to shock the
> people for a time into a sense of insecurity and to put them into a
> frame of mind where they did not differentiate, but seemed to assume
> that the acts of a comparatively few had tainted them all. It was
> government's job to straighten out this situation and do it as quickly as
> possible - and the job is being performed.

This address, which immediately received a favorable public response, has been highly credited for helping to restore public confidence.[63]

2.g. Interpretation and Conclusion

The bank reopening procedure of 1933 was remarkably successful. The bank suspension and reopening performed two major functions; they improved the liquidity of the banking system and assured the solvency of banks that reopened. The first job was achieved by the authorization of Federal Reserve bank notes, and the second through the licensing system which informed the public of the soundness of reopened banks. There are thus two possible explanations for the success: (1) Depositors did not withdraw because they were convinced that the banking system was equipped with enough liquidity to meet potential withdrawal demands; and (2) the public felt safe, being informed that reopened banks had solid financial structures. In this study, the success is attributed to the latter; the licensing system restored public confidence by ensuring that the licensed banks were solvent. The measures taken to supply liquidity did not appear to be adequate considering the severity of the financial trouble.

The licensing scheme, which was at the core of the reopening procedure, furnished information about the soundness of reopened banks.[64] The license informed depositors that the licensed banks had been distinguished from other problem banks. Moreover, the information was verified by governmental authorities having necessary expertise and incentives to be fair. It was this reliable information that reduced depositors' anxiety about banking problems and removed their incentives to withdraw deposits. The government successfully signalled to the public that "bad apples" had already been sorted out, so the "apples" remaining in the "box" were good ones, and hence they are free from epidemics. This information played the key role in overcoming the financial crisis.

In addition, the government effectively communicated its intention to reopen sound banks only and the reopening procedure to the public. This step may be interpreted as providing information in another dimension. One good example is the radio address made by President Roosevelt. He not only emphasized that banks to be reopened would be sound, but also explained how the plan was designed and would work. This augmented the reliability of the information and hence the effectiveness of the licensing scheme.

One may argue that the key to the success was the additional liquidity provided by the government. This argument is hardly convincing. It would have taken a radical measure to tranquilize the intense nationwide bank panic by means of supplying liquidity. This point is well reflected in the proposals and prevailing opinions of that time, which were mostly radical. The most radical one was the nationalization of the whole banking business proposed by the liberals.[65] To subdue the banking panic, government guarantee of deposits was regarded as necessary by the majority of people including bankers, economists, and politicians.[66] The immediate conversion of all government bonds into currency was one of the other proposals considered seriously. Whatever the specific plan might be, it was generally believed to be imperative that the government completely abandon the gold standard and create money on a gigantic scale. In fact, this expectation was one of the reasons for the extraordinary withdrawals of gold that occurred before the moratorium.[67] All these proposals and opinions reflected the severity of the financial crisis and a need for liquidity supply on a huge scale corresponding to the financial condition.

In spite of the perceived need for drastic measures, the Roosevelt administration adopted a moderate plan for the provision of liquidity.[68] The circulating notes issued by the Federal Reserve banks were subject to tax; the Federal Reserve banks had to bear all expenses related to the new currency; collateral requirements were stringent for both Federal Reserve bank notes and loans to banks; the interest charged on the emergency loans was higher than that of normal discounting; The terms of the loan to non-bank institutions were restricted to the maximum of 90 days; and the Federal Reserve System, in its discretion, could discourage banks from borrowing by varying the interest charged on the loan. In sum, the measures adopted to increase liquidity contained numerous safeguards against inflation and were very restrictive considering the severity and complications of the banking problem.

There had been various efforts to furnish liquidity to the banking system even before the national bank holiday. In 1931, the National Credit Corporation was formed. The NCC was funded by voluntary contributions of strong banks. Its efforts to rescue problem banks proved unsuccessful. The government established the Reconstruction Finance Corporation in February 1932. Using funds provided mainly by the Treasury, the RFC made loans to problem banks with relatively liberal collateral requirements.[69] It temporarily decreased the number of bank failures, but failed to restore public confidence.[70] Furthermore, in terms of liquidity supply, the Glass-Steagall Act of 1932 granted the Federal Reserve banks fundamentally similar authorities to those found in the Emergency Banking Act of 1933. In its framework, the act of 1933 was not much different from the act of 1932 which did not show much success. Of course, the Emergency Banking Act enlarged the scale of potential liquidity provision. However, the intensity of the banking crisis increased proportionately far more than the scale of liquidity supply. Therefore, it is implausible that public confidence was restored by virtue of the provision of additional liquidity.

In conclusion, the Roosevelt administration terminated the nationwide bank panic by successfully conveying information about the solvency of banks. Banks differ in their financial strength. Banks that were licensed were ones with sound financial structure. Although the large number of bank failures could be a signal that there were some problem banks, licensed banks were not from that population. It was this information that restored public confidence in banking and stopped the withdrawals of deposits. Therefore, the episode of 1933 convincingly supports the important role of solvency information in bank panics. Depositors were mainly concerned not about the liquidity but about the fundamental solvency of banks. Hence, the fundamental cure for depositors anxiety was to convince them of banks' solvency.

3. THE PANIC OF 1884
IN COMPARISON TO OTHER PANICS

In U.S. history, we can find financial panics of various characteristics and magnitudes. In some cases, bank runs spread very widely and lasted for a considerable period of time, while in other cases, bank panics were both confined to a small geographic area and short-lived. The panic of 1884 is a representative example of the latter. Though the panic was preceded by failures of major financial institutions, it was confined to New York City and lasted for only a brief period.

This section takes a close look at the crisis of 1884 and compares the findings with various aspects of other financial crises.[71] This analysis explains the rather unique case in terms of information costs. The failures of major banks resulted in the panic on a minor scale only because the public distinguished between failed banks and other banks. The banks that failed in 1884 had problems specific to those banks, and the problems were easily noticeable. The unique nature of those problems substantially reduced the cost of bank-specific information and hence made the information available to the public. As a result, depositors were better informed, and did not panic.

3.a. Description of the Panic

The panic of 1873 was followed by a prolonged period of low activity in the stock market and in other branches of the economy. It was not until the beginning of the 1880's that the economy started expanding. Economic activity peaked in 1882, and then declined slowly. Hence, economic conditions preceding the panic of 1884 were characterized by declining economic activity and moderate deflation which had lasted for two years (See Table 5).

As were other financial crises, the panic of 1884 was ignited by failures of major financial institutions. On May 6, 1884, the Marine National Bank of New York City having a capital of $400,000 and deposits of about $5,000,000 closed its doors. The immediate cause of the failure of the bank was the illegal certification of a check for $750,000 for a brokerage firm, Grant & Ward, which had speculated in the stock market. This failure was followed by the failure of Grant & Ward two days later. Due to its reckless speculation, the brokerage firm had a severely impaired capital structure. At the time of its failure, it was estimated that Grant & Ward had assets of less than $700,000 and liabilities of more than $16,000,000. Later, a careful examination by accountants revealed that the firm had assets of $67,174 and liabilities of $16,792,640.[72] The president of the Marine National Bank, James D. Fish, was also a partner of Grant & Ward. Thus, the two financial institutions were very closely connected to each other. Fish's illegal manipulation with bank money was soon learned by bank examiners, and he was sent to the Ludlow Street Jail.[73]

These events undermined the confidence in the financial market and resulted in a severe decline of the stock market. There were growing suspicions and rumors circulating that officers of other banks might be involved in fraudulent banking practices.[74] This suspicion was soon confirmed by another fraud case revealed on May 13. It became known that the president of the Second National Bank of New York City, James C. Eno, had embezzled $3,185,000 of the bank's money and fled to Canada. The directors of the bank immediately replenished the embezzled amount, and the bank managed to avoid suspension or failure. Yet the news was powerful enough to ruin the already shaken confidence in the financial market. The impaired confidence resulted in collapse of stock prices and runs on the banks in New York City.[75]

On the following day, May 14, failures of several brokerage firms, including Nelson Robinson & Co., were announced. The announcement precipitated runs on the Metropolitan National Bank of New York City, whose president was George I. Seney. Seney's two sons and a son-in-law were members of the failed firm, Nelson Robinson & Co., and Seney himself had the reputation of being a large speculator.[76] The bank was compelled to suspend on the same day (May 14). The suspension of one of the major banks in the nation caused great excitements.[77] The price of securities declined further, and banks found it practically impossible to collect their call loans.[78] Subsequently, the suspension was followed by the failures of Atlantic State Bank of Brooklyn, Goffe and Randle, Hatch and Foote, and several other bankers and brokers.

Realizing imminent withdrawal demands, members of the New York Clearing-House Association called an emergency meeting on the afternoon of May 14, and adopted the issuance of clearing house loan certificates. At the same time, the association appointed an *ad hoc* committee for the purpose of examining the asset position of the Metropolitan National Bank and the possibility of its reopening. After its visit to the bank, the committee reported that loan certificates could be safely issued upon most of the securities held by the bank.[79] The solvency of the bank was also confirmed by the examiner dispatched by the Office of the Comptroller of the Currency.[80] Once convinced of the solvency of the bank, the Clearing House Association announced the immediate release of $4 million of loan certificates, most of which were allocated to the Metropolitan National Bank.

Through the assistance rendered by the Clearing House Association, the Metropolitan National Bank was enabled to resume business on the next day following the suspension. Seney resigned from the presidency of the Metropolitan Bank before its reopening. Runs on the Metropolitan bank did not recur after the bank reopened its doors.[81] The stringency of the money market continued for a while. A few more banks and brokerage firms of minor significance, including the Wall Street Bank and G. K. Garrison, failed after the action taken by the Clearing House Association. However, in a few days, the panic subsided (See Table 6 and Table 7 for the recovery of financial conditions). New York banks started gaining currency and gold at the end of May. The *Commercial and Financial Chronicle* reports the recovery as follows:[82]

> June was a month of slow and painful recuperation from the stock panic of May. The banks of New York showed steady and remarkable improvement, and by the end of the month nearly all of the Clearing-House certificates, except those held by the Metropolitan Bank

had been retired, and the surplus reserve above the legal requirement amounted to $13,121,625.[83]

In sum, the financial market experienced exceptional recovery in 1884. The market was disturbed by the failures and suspensions of major financial institutions, and faced great excitements at the initial stage of the crisis. Nevertheless, the banking system avoided devastating results. The panic was terminated within a short period of time. The panic was fairly well confined to the City of New York, and it did not result in a suspension of gold or currency payments, which accompanied most other bank panics.[84]

3.b. Economic Environment

In general, financial crises were preceded by a period of economic boom, characterized by a high level of investment in the production sector and a high level of speculative activity in the financial sector. Banks accommodated the money demand arising from those activities by expanding loans at low interest rates. As a natural result, the financial position of banks became riskier with high leverage ratios and high-risk portfolios. This vulnerable condition invited a financial crisis and a sudden decline in economic activity.

The economic environment preceding the panic of 1884 was atypical. Economic activities peaked in 1882 and slowly declined afterwards. A moderate recession began in 1884. Prices were low, and commercial and financial liquidations were going on for several months.[85] The activity level in the stock market was also low without notable excitements (See Table 8). Sobel describes the atmosphere of the financial market as follows:[86]

> In May, few expected the market to change until the crop reports came out in early autumn. Until then, the market would remain quiet and "dull." Jay Gould was busy with his railroads; there was no sign of a sudden raid from that quarter. Rusell Sage's activities, always watched with care, were also normal. J. P. Morgan was preparing for a European

trip, and William Vanderbilt was engaged in no new enterprise. All the leading figures of American finance and speculation seemed content with the markets and showed no desire to upset the quiet of the city. It was during those humid days of early spring that Ferdinand Ward set into motion a chain of events that would destroy a score of brokerages and shock the nation.

More importantly, the financial position of banks didn't seem vulnerable either in an absolute sense or in comparison with other major panics. Neither overexpansion of loans nor holdings of risky securities were prevalent. Hence, the economic environment was one of the aspects distinguishing the panic of 1884 from others.

3.c. The Development Pattern of the Panic

In most financial panic cases in U.S. history, the first sign of trouble appeared in the form of the failure of some large brokerage firms and banks engaged in risky transactions (See Table 9). The immediate cause of those failures was a sudden decrease in the price of risky assets. The decreased price undermined the asset and liquidity positions of banks that had taken excessive risks by holding risky portfolios. Naturally, the impaired financial position resulted in the failures of those banks. The problem was magnified when such failures undermined public confidence in banks in general. Depositors, when they became suspicious about the solvency of other banks, withdrew deposits compelling banks to liquidate their assets and call in loans. What came next was a further decline of security prices and severe monetary stringency. These results placed more financial institutions in trouble. This process stimulated a diffusion of bank runs; a rise in the price of liquidity called for a higher demand for liquidity by making a larger number of banks desperate for liquidity. This was the general development pattern of financial crises in the United States.

The panic of 1884, which commenced with the failures of the Marine National Bank and the brokerage firm Grant & Ward showed a similar pattern at the beginning. The later developments, however, were different. The failures of the financial institutions, though they were very large ones, did not seriously impair public confidence in 1884. This difference in the magnitude of financial the crisis can be explained by the difference in the cause of failures.

3.d. Causes of Failures

Financial crises have generally been ignited by failure of financial institutions engaged in risky transactions. In most cases, the immediate cause of the failures was a financial problem that might affect a large set of banks given the prevailing economic condition (See Table 9).

In 1837, the panic was precipitated by the failures of cotton businesses. Rising cotton prices in the early 1830's induced an over-investment boom and speculation in cotton. In 1836 and 1837, an economic downturn in Britain resulted in a decreased demand and hence a lower price of cotton.[87] This development led to the failures of numerous commercial and financial institutions that had been involved in the cotton business. Needless to say, cotton was a major agricultural product at that time. Thus, the financial involvement of banks in cotton production was regarded as a common practice.[88]

In the panics of 1857 and 1873, railroad stocks played the major role. Over-investment in railroads, induced by a business boom, lowered their profitability, resulting in a series of failures of railroad companies and a decline in the price of railroad stocks in general. Subsequently, financial institutions failed due to advances made to failed railroad companies or excessive holdings of risky railroad stocks. In the nineteenth century, the railroad was one of the most important industries in the U.S. economy. Knowing that, the public had a good reason to conjecture that the financial condition of most banks in the nation might have been adversely affected by the decreased price of railroad related securities.

The panic of 1893 was caused by monetary disturbances resulting from the Sherman Silver Purchase Act of 1890. The act empowered the Treasury to issue legal tender redeemable in either gold or silver. The authorization of the silver-backed currency broke the adjustment mechanism of the gold standard; an outflow of gold did not necessitate monetary contraction and a lower price level which might turn around the direction of gold flows. At the beginning of the 1890's, gold flows were active due to domestic and international business fluctuations and uncertainty about the maintenance of the gold standard.[89] As usual, gold inflows entailed monetary expansions. However, whenever the nation experienced an outflow of gold, the Treasury offset it by issuing legal tender backed by silver. The Treasury notes authorized in 1890 caused substantial increases in the total amount of U.S. government notes at the beginning of the decade in spite of slight decreases in the amount of gold-backed notes (See Table 10).

Expectations of currency inflation, induced by the Sherman Silver Purchase Act, stimulated speculation during the early 1890's both in the commercial and financial sector.[90] As a result, the average financial condition of the economy became unsound. However, the abundance of legal tender backed by silver enabled banks to maintain sufficient reserves without contracting loans, and thus enabled insolvent business firms to survive longer. Hence, necessary commercial and financial liquidations were delayed. When the crisis came, many banks found that they had been carrying a large amount of loans that should have been written off or at least written down.[91]

The general uneasiness about the currency resulting from the Sherman Silver Act was responsible for the panic of 1893. Sobel describes the situation as follows:[92]

> The Wall Street collapse was a reflection of the nation's monetary

problem. In mid-May [1893] several bankers announced that the silver dollar was worth less than 55 cents in gold, and some New York banks refused to accept them. Notes drawn on Western and Southern banks, which had indicated an unwillingness to settle drafts in gold, were no longer honored in New York, and a wave of failures began in the West, soon to spread throughout the nation.

The Sherman Silver Act was a product of agitation for the free and unlimited coinage of silver. U.S. silver producers in the West and debtor farmers in the Middle West and South had advocated for the free coinage of silver, while mortgage holders in the East had opposed it.[93] Hence, after the passage of the Sherman Silver Act, there was uncertainty about the nation's monetary regime (gold standard or bimetallism). Undoubtedly, such a macroeconomic problem, i.e., the monetary uncertainty, would exert nationwide influence. Because of the belief that the monetary problem might have impaired the soundness of most financial institutions in the nation, the public lost its confidence in the banking system as a whole.[94] Consequently, the financial crisis was nationwide and prolonged (See Table 11).

The failure of an attempt to corner the copper market was the immediate cause of the panic of 1907. The crisis started with runs on the Mercantile National Bank which was involved in an attempted copper corner. Unlike cotton in 1837 or railroads in 1857 and 1873, copper was an industry of relatively minor significance. Hence, normally the event should have not seriously altered public perception toward the solvency of banks in general. Yet it was followed by a series of runs on financial institutions.

Banking developments of the early 1900's explain this anomaly. At the beginning of the decade, some speculative individuals started taking over banking businesses and pursued rapid expansion.[95] Soon they formed a banking circle which financially connected new bankers aggressively seeking expansion. The leaders of the circle included F. A. Heinze, C. W. Morse, O.

F. Thomas, and C. T. Barney. They had control over a large number of commercial and financial institutions, and were financially linked by mutual investment.[96] Heinze was president of Mercantile National Bank and had interests in Consolidated National Bank and a chain of other institutions. Morse, who was a director of the Mercantile National, had control over a dozen banks and trust companies in New York, three in Maine, and two in New Hampshire. Thomas had control over Hamilton Bank, Consolidated National Bank, and Mechanics' and Traders' Bank. Barney was president of Knickerbocker Trust Company and a director of the Trust Company of America. Due to the highly active business style of these individuals, their affiliations were well known in the financial market.

The financial affiliations explain runs on a large number of banks. When the stock of United Copper owned by Heinze collapsed, the influence was not confined to Mercantile National Bank, but extended to all the banks and trust companies belonging in the banking circle. Depositors became suspicious of the soundness of the financial institutions related to the United Copper and Mercantile National Bank. Bank runs were soon disseminated to other financial institutions of the banking chain. Although the importance of copper was minor, the effect appeared to be general due to the financial affiliations among a large number of banks controlled by a few speculative individuals.

In 1884, the cause of failures was rather obvious fraud by the management of the failed financial institutions. The failure of Grant & Ward, the most significant failure that occurred during the crisis, was not a by-product of adverse conditions in the stock market. Though the stock market had declined since 1882, the decline was gradual. There was no great excitement in the stock market, which might have shocked the economy (See Table 12). Instead, the collapse of Grant & Ward was a product of reckless speculation and fraud by a partner of the firm, Ferdinand Ward. Sobel (1968), describes Ward's reckless speculation as follows:[97]

Together with Fish and others, he was speculating heavily on the Stock Exchange. Their choices were poor; Ward was a bull when he should have switched to the bear side, and plunged heavily into several situations that went sour.

Given this exceptional behavior of Ward, it was rather obvious that the problem was specific to Grant & Ward.

The Marine National failed due to its major financial involvement with Grant & Ward. The bank made a huge amount of loans to Grant & Ward mostly on the firm's unprotected notes. According to Kane, the firm carried three accounts with the bank, a private account of one member of the firm, a general account, and a special account. Many of the notes for which the firm was liable were in the names of clerks employed by the firm, of no financial standing, and relatives of one of its members.[98] Fish, president of the Marine National, was also a partner in Grant & Ward. Given this relation, the public could easily understand the specific connection between the bank and the brokerage firm.

It was also apparent that the embezzlement by president of the Second National Bank was not a reflection of general banking condition, but merely a product of personal misbehavior. Examiners reported to the Comptroller that the president used the money in speculations in Wall Street, and was able to conceal the fact of his misappropriation of the funds of the bank on account of the securities being kept in a vault located at some distance from the regular banking rooms. The president had access to those securities without check or hinderance, and used them to obtain money for his own private speculation.[99]

One remaining question is how a fraud on such a large scale, large enough to shock the whole nation, was possible in the sophisticated financial market of the time. Of course, fraud in the financial market is not such a rare event. However, even in the 19th century, the financial market was sophisticated enough not to be fooled on such a large scale as the sum of over 16 millions.

That kind of fraud would not be possible in normal circumstances. The explanation can be found in a unique "advantage" possessed by Grant & Ward.

The brokerage firm, Grant & Ward, was formed as a partnership by Ulysses Grant Jr. and Ferdinand Ward in 1880. Ward, who had started his career at Wall Street at a very young age, was a daring speculator having extraordinary persuasive powers.[100] On the other hand, Grant was a naive young man of mediocre ability. The significance of the story is rooted in the background of Grant. Grant was a son of the former president of the United States, Ulysses S. Grant, who was in office during the years between 1869 and 1877. U. S. Grant himself joined the firm later as a limited partner.

Ward shrewdly took advantage of the Grant connection in defrauding investors. At first, Ward speculated with the capital invested by his young partner Grant. He was suffering losses due to reckless speculation. In order to make up the loss, he started borrowing money from people in the financial market, promising profits far in excess of any legitimate or honest returns in any branch of business.[101] A specimen of his promise is found in Collman:[102]

> Feb. 1, 1884
>
> This is to certify that we have this day received from Captain E. Spicer, Jr., $50,000; which we are to invest for him, and we agree to return him said $50,000 May 15, 1884, together with $5,000 profit.
>
> Grant & Ward

Ward kept losing the borrowed money in the stock market and paid the interest with newly borrowed money. The rate of return promised by Ward was the kind of offer to which any experienced investor would not even pay attention in normal circumstances. Nevertheless, Ward was successful in convincing investors that the extraordinary rates of return were possible by virtue of Grant's connections. According to Ward, he controlled firms that had large and highly profitable government contracts obtained through Grant's influence. These contracts supposedly would yield 10 to 20 percent a month.[103] Needless to say, such contracts never existed. Fish, president of the Marine National, was an example of someone lured by the Grant connection. The *Nation* reported that Fish had tried to confirm the profitability of the firm's investment with General Grant before he became involved with Grant & Ward by discounting the firm's notes in the amount of $200,000. However, he was misled by ambiguous responses of General Grant. On July 5, 1882, Fish made an inquiry by writing a letter to General Grant. He said that the amount was not trifling for him and added:[104]

> It is necessary that the credit of Grant & Ward should deservedly stand very high. These notes, as I understand it, are given for no other purpose than to raise money for the payment of grain, etc., purchased to fill the Government contracts. Under the circumstances, my dear General, you will see that it is of most vital importance to me particularly that the credit of the firm shall always be untarnished and unimpaired. I will be happy to meet you at almost any time you may name to talk these matters over.

The following was the personal response by General Grant dated July 6, 1882:

> My Dear Mr. Fish:
> On my arrival in the city this A. M., I find your letter of yesterday with a letter from Thomas L. James, President of the Lincoln Nation Bank, and copy of your reply to the letter. Your understanding in regard to our liabilities in the firm of Grant & Ward is the same as mine. If you desire it I am entirely willing that the advertisement of the firm shall be so changed as to express this. Not having been in the city for more than a week, I have a large accumulated mail to look over, and some business appointments to meet, so that I may not be able to get down to see you to-day. But if I can I will go before 3 o'clock.

Very truly yours,

In addition to this personal letter, a formal letter was sent on the same day to Fish from the office of the firm:[105]

My Dear Mr. Fish:
In relation to the matter of discount kindly made by you for account of Grant & Ward, I would say that I think the investments are safe, and I am willing that Mr. Ward should derive what profit he can for the firm that the use of my name and influence may bring.

Yours very truly,

This story tells us that Grant & Ward would not have been able to shock the nation without its unique "advantage," namely, the Grant connection.

In sum, the cause of the failures that occurred in 1884 was specific to the financial institutions directly involved. This circumstance distinguishes the panic of 1884 from other financial crises involving more general causes.

3.e. Perception of the Public

The development of a panic greatly depends on the public perception of the state of the banking sector. If depositors conjecture that banks in general are experiencing financial difficulties, they will withdraw deposits. Banking problems are then precipitated regardless of the actual condition of banks.

It appears that the public did not have a feeling of crisis in 1884. The attitude of the public can be inferred from opinions and statements found in various sources. Some of them are introduced for the purpose of illustration.

In fact, merchants here and everywhere, and bankers and brokers in other cities, except in case of some direct connection, have looked almost with indifference upon our bank failures and wild scramble in

Wall Street. They are fully conscious of its local, sporadic character.
Commercial and Financial Chronicle, Vol.38, p.581

It should be remembered that this has not been strictly speaking a
financial nor a commercial panic, but a moral panic. Commercially we
were in a conservative condition, and financially we were by no means
extended; on the contrary, capital was abundant, interest was low, and
merchants were comparatively out of debt.
Commercial and Financial Chronicle, Vol.38, p.629

If anybody who never witnessed a panic before supposed that what he
saw on Wednesday week in Wall Street was a repetition or renewal of
the panics of 1857 or 1873, he was greatly mistaken. Those were
veritable commercial crises of the first order. The scenes of Wednesday
were very exciting and very alarming to the ordinary investor, but they
were not in any way indications that we were entering on such a period
of disaster as followed the failure of the Ohio Life and Trust Company
in 1857, or that of Jay Cooke & Co. in 1873.
Nation, 1884, p.440

Because a few banks have suffered from mismanagement they ought
not to suspect all banking institutions.
There has been no sudden deterioration in the morals of men, or in the
conduct of corporations whereby confidence in them should be
withdrawn entirely.
Whether we have reached the end or not can not be predicted. One
thing is certain, however, these speculative losses are not injurious to
general business. On the other hand, its improvement will come all the
more quickly through quenching the fires of speculation.
Bankers' Magazine (New York), Vol.39, pp.901, 902, 905.

the atmosphere in May 1884 was not as gloomy as it had been after the
first days of the 1837, 1857, and 1873 panics. The country was not
fearful of a general collapse. Instead, interested observers seemed to sit
back and wonder who would fall next.
Sobel, p.220

These quotes show that the bank failures of 1884 did not significantly alter the public perception of the soundness of the banking system as a whole. This relatively minor effect of bank failures on public perception is explained by the economic environment and by the cause of failures that differentiated the 1884 panic from others.

3.f. Interpretation

The panic of 1884 is distinguished from other panics by the preceding economic environment and the cause of the bank failures. In effects, events presented the public with bank specific information. It was this information that prevented the panic from spreading widely.

Financial failures can be a strong signal of distress within the financial sector when the general economic condition also indicates a vulnerable condition of the financial market. Similarly, failures caused by an event affecting the financial market in general may signal problems for financial institutions in general. Depositors receiving this signal can hardly be certain whether the asset position of a particular bank has become unfavorable unless the financial condition of the bank was verified in advance. Provided that it is very costly for depositors to analyze the asset portfolio of a bank, they would be better off by simply withdrawing deposits.

This signalling effect of bank failures was not pronounced in 1884. The panic of 1884 was rather unique. Although depositors were initially alarmed by the failures of the Marine National and Grant & Ward, and by the subsequent embezzlement case of the Second National Bank, they soon learned the unique nature of failures. The public understood that the problems were confined to specific financial institutions, and that the failures did not indicate an adverse condition in the financial market. It was this knowledge that enabled the public to maintain its composure.

Fraud may be regarded as exceptional behavior. Even if it is not an exception, fraud of some individuals does not indicate that others in general behave in the same way. Depositors' suspicion about other banks would not arise from failures of some banks that had been managed in an extraordinary manner. Thus, depositors remained calm when the failures of the Marine National and Grant & Ward were announced. However, upon learning of another fraud case of the Second National Bank, the public became confused, thinking that fraud might be more widespread than expected. Depositors started withdrawing deposits from Metropolitan National Bank whose financial structure was deemed to be impaired. The bank was connected with a failed brokerage firm, and its president had the reputation of being a large speculator. They conjectured that speculators were more likely to be involved in fraud. The bank was compelled to suspend. In order to ascertain the financial condition of the Metropolitan, the Clearing House Association and the Comptroller of the Currency dispatched examiners to the bank. The examiners reported that the bank was solvent. This examination result confirmed the initial public belief that fraud was not such a common practice in the financial market. Depositors easily regained their confidence. There were no more runs on the Metropolitan after it resumed business. The financial crisis was over.

The interpretation of this development is as follows. In 1884, the failed banks had rather obvious and unique problems, so it was relatively easy for depositors to distinguish failed banks from other banks in terms of their financial strength. In other words, bank-specific information was available at low cost. The low cost enabled the public to be better informed. Thus, the availability of information at low cost was the main reason why the panic was both confined to New York City and short-lived.

3.g. Alternative Interpretations

One variable which should be correlated with the magnitude of a panic is the size of the financial institutions whose failure triggered the panic. Failures of minor financial institutions would not exert a far-reaching effect. Hence, a disturbance triggered by minor failures should quickly subside without causing serious problems. The panic of 1884 definitely does not resemble such a situation. Even in comparison with the financial institutions involved in other major bank panics, the financial institutions failed in 1884 were of major size (See Table 13). The liabilities of Grant & Ward, which were over $16 million, were significant by any standard. Moreover, the amount eventually defaulted on, which almost equaled total liabilities, might be unprecedented.

The explanation most frequently adopted by bank panic literature is that the prompt action by the Clearing House Association tranquilized the panic. The argument is that the early issuance of clearing house loan certificates quickly restored public confidence in the liquidity of banks and prevented further bank runs. This interpretation overlooks some important factors. The clearing house loan certificates can be used only for interbank settlements. Accordingly, they do not increase the amount of reserves of the banking system as a whole, which can be used to meet the withdrawals of currency for hoarding. Hence, the loan certificates are not such a powerful device when the public loses confidence in the banking system as a whole. Moreover, the amount of certificates was limited to $4 million in 1884, most of which was planned to be issued to the Metropolitan National Bank. This information was public. Hence, if the public had lost its confidence in the banking system as a whole, more suspensions of other banks would have followed.

To some extent, clearing house loan certificates contributed to restoring public confidence. However, their contribution was not through enhancing the liquidity of the banking system but through verifying the solvency of Metropolitan National Bank. The verification was very effective thanks to the abundance of already existing information. Therefore, it is fallacious to argue that the early issuance of clearing house loan certificates and the resulting liquidity enhancement played a major role in stopping the bank runs.

3.h. Conclusion

Bank panics were the most widely spread and prolonged when it was difficult for depositors to recognize the difference in the financial strength of banks (e.g. the panic of 1893). In 1884, the problems of failed financial institutions were so conspicuous that depositors could easily distinguish the failed ones from the rest. Their ability to do so stopped them from running on banks in general. Hence, bank-specific information available at a low cost was the main reason for the small magnitude of the panic in 1884. The episodes of U.S. panics that we have examined show that a better informed public is less likely to panic.

In addition, the unique experience of 1884 answers an important question. The question is if fraud can be a major disturbance in the financial market. Even if depositors make banks provide their financial information by strongly demanding it, the public may not be able to detect fraudulent behavior which is deliberately concealed. Then fraud may produce unexpected failures. If such failures are contagious, the provision of information cannot prevent financial troubles caused by illegal banking practices. However, the episode of 1884 suggests that failures resulting from fraud may not be contagious since the prevalence of fraud can be rather independent among individuals. Therefore, provided that sound banks find effective means to prove their financial strength, they should be able to prevent the contagion of bank failures.

4. SUMMING-UP

The first two sections of this chapter have analyzed the methods used to manage financial crises. The analyses show that the effectiveness of a method was mainly a function of providing information. In U.S. history, banks and the government tranquilized bank panics by providing financial information on banks, rather than by improving the liquidity position of banks.

The last section has concentrated on the cost of information. Bank failures were more contagious when they were caused by a more general cause. On the other hand, bank failures caused by a problem specific to the failed institutions did not exert a far-reaching effect. In the latter case, it was not difficult, i.e., not costly, for depositors to distinguish the failed banks from sound banks in business. As a result, depositors were well equipped with bank-specific information, and hence did not panic.

In sum, bank panics were stopped by providing information and prevented when information was relatively abundant. Therefore, bank failure contagion is an information problem. More specifically, the contagion is caused by the lack of bank-specific information.

NOTES

1. Bank failures may affect the solvency of the banking system as a whole if they substantially decrease the price of less liquid assets. However, this effect materializes after depositors start running on banks in general. Hence, such a systemwide problem is rather a result than a cause of the bank panic.
2. Comptroller of the Currency. *Annual Report*, Washington: Government Printing Office, 1893, p.16; Sprague, O. *History of the Crisis under the National Banking System*, Washington: Government printing Office, 1910, p.47.
3. Since the establishment of the New York Clearing House Association in 1853, clearing house loan certificates were used to manage almost all minor and major panics including those of 1873, 1884, 1893, and 1907.
4. Sprague, 1910, pp.46, 49.
5. Kane, Thomas. *The Romance and Tragedy of Banking*, New York: Bankers Publishing Co., 1923, p.118; Sprague, 1910, p.113.
6. On May 14, 1884, the following plan was adopted in an emergency meeting of the members of the New York Clearing House Association (Comptroller of the Currency, 1884, p.33):

    Resolved, That, in view of the present crisis, the banks in the association, for the purpose of sustaining each other and the business community, resolve: That a committee of five be appointed by the chair, to receive from banks members of the association bills receivable and other securities to be approved by said committee, who shall be authorized to issue therefor to such depositing banks certificates of deposit bearing interest at six per cent. per annum not in excess of 75 per cent. of the securities or bills receivable so deposited, except in case of United States bonds, and said certificates shall be received in settlement of balances at the clearing house.

    The arrangements were similar in other banking panic cases, though there were some minor differences such as the interest rate born by the certificates, redemption period, the maximum percentage allowed to be issued on securities, and the maximum total amount.
7. Comptroller of the Currency, 1884, pp.36, 37.

8. *Commercial and Financial chronicle, and Hunt's Merchants' Magazine*, New York: William B. Dona and Co., 1873, Vol. 17, p.411.
9. *Commercial and Financial Chronicle*, 1873, Vol.17, p.448.
10. "Briefly stated, they [clearing house loan certificates] were temporary loans made by banks associated together as a clearing-house association to the members of such association, and were available to such banks only for the purpose of settling balances due from and to each other, these balances under normal conditions of business being settled in coin or currency" (Comptroller of the Currency, 1893, pp.15, 16).
11. The arrangements adopted by the New York banks in the Clearing House association, on Sep. 20, 1873, include the following (Comptroller of the Currency, 1873, p.27):

    That in order to accomplish the purpose set forth in the arrangement the legal tender belonging to the associated banks shall be considered and treated as a common fund, held for mutual aid and protection, and the committee appointed shall have the power to equalize the same by assessment or otherwise, at their discretion.
12. *Commercial and Financial Chronicle*, 1873, Vol.17, p.177.
13. *Bankers' Magazine and Statistical Register*, New York: Homans Publishing Co., 1873, Vol.8, p.235. The July issue of the same magazine (Vol.8, p.156) also expressed concern over money market matters:

    The usual condition of ease marks the period of midsummer in the money market. The balances of country banks continue to accumulate, and loans on calls are made at low rates. The ordinary course of events will doubtlessly prevail; full sail will be carried as if summer were to last forever, and when the now plethoric accounts are diminished by their owners, sharp and sudden calls will damage not merely stock speculations but legitimate business throughout the country.
14. This was a substantial underestimation. According to *Commercial and Financial Chronicle* (1873, Vol.17, p.71), the average cost per mile in the U.S. was $55,116.
15. Reopen on September 30.
16. *Nation*, New York: E. L. Godkin and Co., 1873, p.216.

17. Sprague, 1910, pp.50, 51.

18. *Bankers' Magazine* (see n.13), 1873, Vol.8, p.325.

19. Derived from a table in Sprague (1910, p.52).

20. *Commercial and Financial Chronicle*, 1873, Vol.17, p.411.

21. On September 26, *Commercial and Financial Chronicle* (1873, Vol.17, p.429) reported:
    The financial disorders referred to in our last having increased in violence, and extended to all the principal cities and towns of the United States, have been felt with considerable force in mercantile circles.

22. *Bankers' Magazine: Journal of Money Market, and Commercial Digest*, London: Waterlow and Sons, 1873, p.996.

23. *Bankers' Magazine* (see n.13, Vol.8, p.404) reported:
    The money market has been in a continued state of excitement throughout the month of October. The failures of numerous bankers in September and October have lessened confidence as to the position of firms hitherto in first-class credit. The drain upon currency in Wall Street Continued for several weeks, for account of Western and Southern bankers, who have had to sustain a severe pressure for the past six weeks from their own depositors.

24. Comptroller of the Currency, 1873, p.30.

25. *Commercial and Financial Chronicle*, 1873, Vol.17, p.547.

26. *Commercial and Financial Chronicle*, 1873, Vol.17, p.793.

27. *Commercial and Financial Chronicle* (1873, Vol.17, p.447) reported the conflict of interests associated with the equalization of reserves:
    the question whether the banks ought any longer to pool their greenbacks as they have done for the last fortnight. Some of strong banks would become stronger, while the weak banks would become weaker by a separation. The former, therefore, are some of them anxious to break ranks, the latter to hold fast together.

28. "In none of earlier [prior to 1933] episodes, with possible exception of the restriction that began in 1839 and continued until 1842, was there any extensive series of bank failures after restriction [of payments] occurred." Friedman, Milton and Schwartz, Anna J. *A Monetary History of the United States, 1867-1960*, Princeton: University Press, 1963, p.329.

29. Sprague, 1910, p.280.
30. "Restriction of payment [of 1907] thus protected the banking system and gave time for the immediate panic to wear off, as well as for additional currency to be made available." Friedman and Schwartz, 1910, p.167.
31. The Office of the Comptroller of the Currency and the Clearing House Association; the Federal Reserve banks after their establishment.
32. Comptroller of the Currency, 1873, p.10.
33. Federal Reserve Board. *Annual Report*, Washington: Government Printing Office, 1933, p.3. Although the banking was unstable also in the 1920's due to rapid expansion, the average annual rate of suspension during the decade was 2.1 percent. Upham, Cyril and Lamke, Edwin. *Closed and Distressed Banks*, Washington: Brookings Institutions, Washington D.C., 1934, p.247.
34. U.S. Department of the Commerce. *Historical Statistics of the United States: 1789-1945,* Washington: Government Printing Office, 1949. This figure excludes the suspensions under a special banking holiday declared by the civil authorities.
35. Nadler, Marcus and Bogen, Jules. *The Banking Crisis: The End of an Epoch*, New York: Dodd, Mead and Company, 1933, p.146.
36. Nadler and Bogen, 1933, p.152.
37. Federal Reserve Board(see n.33), 1933, p.8. For reference, on Dec. 30, 1933, money in circulation and the reserve balances were $5,806,000,000 and $2,677,693,000 respectively (*Ibid*, pp.141, 164).
38. O'Connor, J. *The Banking Crisis and Recovery under the Roosevelt Administration*, Chicago: Callaghan and Company, 1938. The full texts of proclamation and executive orders issued by the President in connection with the banking emergency are found in the appendix of the book. The appendix also provides the transcripts of the regulations issued by the Treasury Department.
39. Kennedy, Susan. *The Banking Crisis of 1933*, Lexington: University Press of Kentucky, 1973, pp.166, 167.
40. Burns, Helen. *The American Banking Community and New Deal Banking Reform: 1933-1935*, Westport: Greenwood Press, 1974, pp.42, 43.
41. Burns, 1974, p.45.

42. Kennedy, 1973, p.170.

43. Kennedy, 1973, p.174.

44. Section 2 of the Act contains the following paragraph:

During time of war or during any other period of national emergency declared by the President, the President may, through any agency he may designate, or otherwise, investigate, regulate, or prohibit, under such rules and regulations as he may prescribe, by means of licenses or otherwise, any transactions in foreign exchange, transfers of credit between or payments by banking institutions as defined by the President, ---.

45. Federal Reserve Board(see n.33), 1933, p.14.

46. Federal Reserve Board. *Federal Reserve Bulletin*, Washington: U.S. Government Printing Office, 1933, p.209.

47. Federal Reserve Board (see n.33), 1933, p.15.

48. O'Connor, 1938, p.20.

49. O'Connor, 1938, p.19.

50. Upham and Lamke, 1934, p.48.

51. Sec. 203 of the Act states:

Whenever he shall deem it necessary in order to conserve the assets of any bank for the benefit of the depositors and other creditors thereof, the Comptroller of the Currency may appoint a conservator for such bank and require of him such bond and security as the Comptroller of the Currency deems proper.

Previously, the Comptroller of the Currency was authorized to appoint a receiver who could only liquidate problem banks.

52. O'Connor, 1938, pp.42-47; Upham and Lamke, 1934, pp.70-74.

53. The Reconstruction Finance Corporation was a major buyer of the preferred stocks issued for bank reorganization. In addition, the Banking Act of 1933 eliminated the double liability of bank share holders to facilitate the reorganization by means of issuing equity shares.

54. This method required the assent of creditors owning 75 % of the liabilities.

55. O'Connor, 1938, p.87.

56. Section 18 of the Federal Reserve Act of 1913.

57. Sec. 404 of the Act states:

    any state bank or trust company not a member of the Federal Reserve
    System may apply to the Federal Reserve Bank in the district in
    which it is located and said Federal Reserve Bank, in its discretion
    and after inspection and approval of collateral and a thorough
    examination of the applying bank or trust company, may make direct
    loans to such state bank or trust company under the terms provided
    in Section 10 (b) of the Federal Reserve Act, ---.

58. Section 13 of the Federal Reserve Act of 1913.

59. Federal Reserve Board (see n.33), 1933, pp.15, 102.

60. Lindley, Ernest. *The Roosevelt Revolution*, New York: Viking Press,
    1933, p.93.

61. The currency created by the Emergency Banking Act was commonly
    known as Federal Reserve bank notes as opposed to Federal Reserve
    notes.

62. Roosevelt, Franklin. *On Our Way*, New York: John Day Company,
    1934, pp.26-34. The full text of this address is found in the book.

63. Kennedy, 1973, p.181.

64. "An important purpose of this action [national bank holiday] was to
    attack the problem of bank failures comprehensively by reviewing at
    one time the condition of all banks and reopening only such banks as
    could meet all demands upon them" [Federal Reserve Board (see n.33),
    1933, p.10].

65. Burns, 1974, p.72; Kennedy, 1973, p.167.

66. Nadler and Bogen, 1933, p.136; Kennedy, 1973, p.166.

67. Sullivan, Lawrence. *Prelude to Panic*, Washington: Statesman Press,
    1936, pp.42, 43, 78.

68. Roosevelt advocated "conventional banking method," and Woodin,
    secretary of the Treasury, was described as conservative "hard money"
    man (Burns, 1974, pp.100, 105).

69. Upham and Lamke, 1934, p.8.

70. "Numerous recipients of RFC funds failed. Of 65 banks in Chicago
    which borrowed from the RFC up to July 20, 1932, only 18 remained
    open in February 1933" (Upham and Lamke, 1934, p.156).

71. Attention will be paid mainly to the panics occurred between 1863 and 1913, which is the period after the establishment of national banking system and before Federal Reserve system. Outside this period, the financial regime is believed to have been different.

72. Sobel, Robert. *Panic on Wall Street: A History of American Financial Disasters*, New York: Macmillan Company, 1968, p.222.

73. Sobel, 1968, p.218.

74. *Commercial and Financial Chronicle*, 1884, Vol.38, p.589.

75. *Commercial and Financial Chronicle*, 1884, Vol.38, p.589.

76. Kane, 1923, p.118; Sobel, 1968, p.219.

77. Metropolitan National Bank had capital of $3,000,000. In 1884, the average amount of capital of the national banks in New York City was about $1,060,000, and that of all national banks was about $201,000. The averages have been derived from statistics in Comptroller of the Currency (1884).

78. Comptroller of the Currency, 1884, p.33.

79. Comptroller of the Currency, 1884, pp.33, 34.

80. Comptroller of the Currency, 1884, p.42.

81. Sobel, 1968, p.221.

82. *Commercial and Financial Chronicle*, 1884, Vol.39, p.7.

83. All of the loan certificates had been rendered and canceled by July 1, except those issued to the Metropolitan National Bank (Comptroller of the Currency, 1884, p.37).

84. The issue of the loan certificates was confined to the banks of New York City.

85. Comptroller of the Currency, 1884, p.34.

86. Sobel, 1968, p.209.

87. Lightner, Otto. *The History of Business Depressions*, New York: Northeastern Press, 1922, p.126.

88. Nicholas Biddle, who had been president of the Second Bank of the United States and one of leading bankers in the nation, attempted to corner the cotton market and issued currency against the crops (Sobel, 1968 p.70).

89. Friedman and Schwartz, 1963, p.104.

90. Sobel, 1968, p.240.

91. Sprague, 1910, p.161.

92. Sobel, 1968, p.252.
93. Friedman and Schwartz, 1963, pp.113-119.
94. Kane (1923, p.198) describes the cause of the panic as follows:
   It [the panic of 1893] had its origin, as Mr Eckels [Comptroller of the Currency in 1893] stated, in a loss of confidence in the solvency of the banks, and this loss of confidence was inspired by a general knowledge of the unsound conditions in private and in public life, described by Mr. Lacey [Comptroller of the Currency in 1991] in his report for 1891, and the speculative and venturesome character of the investments and loans in which the funds of many of the banks had been risked.
95.   In January, 1901, he bought the Produce Exchange Bank and the Bank of New Amsterdam. By April, he obtained the Twelfth Ward Bank; seven days later, the Bank of the State of New York; in October, the national Broadway. Seventeen days after, he was owner of the national Commercial; in December he possessed the National Bank of North America. Two days later, Morse won his ninth New York bank, the Fourteenth Street; within ten months he owned interests in the Trust Company of America and the Van North Trust Company.

   He was using the stock and surplus of one bank in order to buy the next one. He was hypothecating and rehypothecating his securities in depositories in New England.

   Collman. Charles. *Our Mysterious Panics, 1830-1930*, New York: William Morrow and Co., 1931, pp.228, 229.
96. Collman, 1931, pp.228-231; Sprague, 1910, pp.246-253.
97. Sobel, 1968, p.212.
98. Kane, 1923, p.123.
99. Comptroller of the Currency, 1884, p.43.
100. Sobel, 1968, pp.209, 210.
101. *Nation*, 1884, p.420.
102. Collman, 1931, p.127.
103. *Nation*, 1884, p.461.
104. *Nation*, 1884, p.460.

105. *Nation*, 1884, pp.460, 461. After the firm failed, Grant claimed that
     he did not scrutinize this formal letter, but signed it on the assurance
     that it was only an ordinary letter in the course of business (*Ibid*,
     p.458).

CHAPTER V

Related Issues

In order to avoid digression and resulting disorderliness, previous chapters have concentrated on the triggering mechanism of bank panics and have not dealt with other related issues. As a result, some questions may remain unanswered. This chapter briefly discusses those issues.

1. COLLECTIVE EFFORTS AND BANKS' BEHAVIOR

When the government or banks repetitively adopt collective efforts to manage bank panics, the collective efforts can be equivalent to an established lender of last resort. In other words, banks can anticipate that help will come in an emergency. Hence, it is worthwhile to consider if measures used by the clearing house might have effects on the behavior of banks.

Equalization of reserves is a problem sharing scheme. The importance of liquidity is pronounced in a financial crisis. If reserves are shared in an emergency, the high liquidity of an individual bank is not rewarded. Hence, the anticipation of reserve pooling would create an opportunity to free-ride and hence discourage banks from maintaining high liquidity. This incentive to free-ride can make the banking system more vulnerable. Given its poor information content and the free-rider problem, equalization of reserves does not appear to be a viable scheme.

Clearing house loan certificates can also cause the same problem when they are used unconditionally, i.e., regardless of the solvency of banks. Undoubtedly, it is more profitable for banks to hold interest bearing securities than to hold legal tender. The loan certificates enable banks to use securities in lieu of legal tender in an emergency. Thus, the banks that anticipate the issuance of clearing house loan certificates would minimize reserve holdings.

However, the free-rider problem may not be as serious with the loan certificates as with equalization of reserves. The loan certificates differ from equalization of reserves in that they are not a perfect substitute for legal tender; they were used only for interbank settlements, and the amount issued was substantially smaller than the face value of securities - 75% in most cases. More importantly, it is possible to charge a penalty rate on the loan certificates. The ability to impose the penalty may critically depend on the solvency of banks to which the loan certificates are issued. Insolvent banks do not have much to lose, while solvent banks face the possibility of bank failure contagion. Hence, the bargaining power between insolvent banks and solvent ones seems to be unbalanced; that is, insolvent banks can adopt a tougher strategy. This might prevent solvent banks from penalizing insolvent ones. The situation is different if the clearing house issues the certificates only to solvent members merely experiencing liquidity problems. Such solvent banks face the danger of imminent failure and hence of losing their equity. This problem would probably outweigh the problem of other solvent banks, i.e., the possibility of failure contagion. Furthermore, the loan certificates enable less liquid banks to prove their fundamental solvency in addition to enhancing liquidity. Given these factors, banks having high liquidity should be able to penalize less liquid banks by charging a high interest rate. This ability can prevent the free-rider problem. In sum, the loan certificates, if used appropriately, may avoid serious free-rider problems.

In U.S. history, the clearing house issued the loan certificates when depositors ran on solvent banks. Insolvent banks, which failed at the initial stage of a panic, were not allowed to obtain the loan certificates. They were issued at a relatively early stage of the panic in 1884. However, in this case, the New York Clearing House Association made the decision after confirming the solvency of the Metropolitan National Bank which was the major beneficiary. This policy of the clearing house appears to have been successful. The contemporary literature on banking shows few records of criticism of the loan certificates by theoreticians or complaints by bankers.

The analysis of this section and the importance of solvency information suggest a desirable role of the lender of last resort. Whether it is private or governmental, the lender of last resort should confine its role to managing occasional liquidity problems faced by sound banks only. This policy will not only improve general welfare but also increase the effectiveness of the lender of last resort. The economy can avoid moral hazard problems, the cost of assisting insolvent banks, and unnecessary welfare losses resulting from failures of solvent institutions. Furthermore, when such policy is publicly understood, assistance rendered by the lender of last resort conveys solvency information and hence greatly facilitates the restoration of public confidence during an emergency.

2. WAYS OF PROVIDING INFORMATION

Bank assets consist of information-intensive items (e.g., loans) whose book value may substantially differ from the market value. Naturally, the evaluation of banks' financial standing involves many difficulties, that is, it is costly to process the financial data of banks. Given these difficulties, mere disclosure of banks' balance sheets does not provide much information. Small depositors would not be willing to bear the cost of information. Hence, in order to effectively communicate to depositors, banks would have to translate complicated information into a simple form. This section discusses possible ways that banks can provide information.

One possibility is that banks contract a neutral outside party to evaluate their financial information and translate such information into a simple form. In order for the information to be credible, the third party would have to be a well established organization that is concerned about its own reputation. It may be either an established accounting firm or a group of accountants specialized in evaluating bank assets. Such an agency may rate banks based on their soundness. Analogous to this scheme are bond-rating agencies such as Standard & Poor's and Moody's. Triple A banks, being rated as the soundest, would pay the lowest interest rate on deposits. A higher interest rate would be offered by single A banks. The absence of the rating on a bank would imply that the financial standing of the bank was very poor. Then the poorly rated bank would have to offer a substantially higher interest rate to attract depositors. In this situation, the failure of an unrated or very poorly rated bank may not trigger runs on highly rated banks. The recent decline of the junk bond (unrated bond) market did not disturb the bond market in general.

Alternatively, banks with a similar risk may form a coalition. Presumably, it is easier for depositors to understand the credit-worthiness of a coalition than to process the financial data of individual banks. Hence, the membership of a particular coalition can serve as the rating of a member bank. Information provided in this way can be reliable to depositors since member banks have incentives to watch each other. They have to preserve the reputation of their coalition and prevent the contagion caused by failures of other member banks. Hence, the coalition can be an effective way of providing information if it works properly. Clearing house association may be viewed as a historical example of the coalition which enabled member banks to enjoy a good reputation.

The practicality of this scheme is somewhat controversial. One argument against the coalition is based on a conflict of interest among member banks. Goodhart (1988) argues that it is problematic for banks to reveal information to their competitors and regulate each other.[1] Those banks in charge of the key "club committees" have incentives to take advantage of the information on their competitors and set regulations that would benefit themselves at the expense of others. In addition, close monitoring would be intolerable between competing members. This conflict of interest, he argues, called for a neutral third party and hence naturally induced an emergence of the central bank.

Another problem with the coalition is that it can act as a cartel. A banking coalition may succeed in capturing the dominant market share by establishing an unsurpassed reputation. In this case, the member banks may hinder the entry into the coalition and in effect into the banking industry, and collude against depositors and borrowers. In addition, such a cartel can be more stable than most cartels of other industries. Most cartels are fragile due to incentives to "chisel" and the lack of effective means to penalize "chiselers." Hence, chiseling by a few firms can break the cartel and restore competition. However, the banking cartel can effectively penalize chiselers by excluding them from the coalition. The excluded banks would not be perceived as safe as they had been. Given the importance of information provided by the coalition, the exclusion can even be a "death sentence." This ability to penalize chiselers may make the collusion of banks more successful. The associated welfare costs would then be significant. Therefore, government regulation may be both economically and politically preferred to a voluntary banking coalition that has monopoly power.

The question is if any coalition can enjoy such monopoly power. If the higher reputation is associated with the larger size, one coalition may dominate the banking sector. The existence of such an association is doubtful. Information provided by means of the coalition is credible only when the member banks can effectively monitor each other. The effective monitoring requires familiarity and cooperation among the member banks. Given these requirements, a larger coalition may not have an advantage in providing information. There may exist an optimal size of the coalition.[2] If the optimal size is not exceedingly large, several coalitions may coexist and offer close enough substitutes to depositors and borrowers. In reality, depositors tend to perceive a larger bank to be safer. However, the main reason for this perception of depositors may be that large institutions are more likely to be rescued by the government that fears the repercussion effects from the failure of a large institution.[3] Hence, it is uncertain if large size would be an advantage in a competitive environment.

The major argument for the coalition is that banks have an informational advantage in evaluating bank assets, that is, it is banks that know other banks best. This informational advantage enables banks effectively to monitor each other. This idea was supported by the Comptroller of the Currency in 1907:[4]

> For several years past there has been an increased tendency on the part of all banks to make independent examination in addition to those made by the national-bank examiners. This is considered most desirable, and has been encouraged in every way by the Comptroller's office. Within the last year or two such examinations have been inaugurated by some of the clearing-house associations in the large cities. So far the trial of this system has been very satisfactory, and it is therefore recommended

to the consideration of the clearing-house cities of the country as a means by which better methods of banking can be attained.

The examination by a national-bank examiner and the power of the Comptroller's office are necessarily more or less limited to the discovery of specific violations of the national-bank act, and criticisms and recommendations of the Comptroller's office can not always be made sufficiently mandatory. The information acquired by clearing-house committees, through their own examiners, has in many cases resulted in their being able to enforce better methods and more conservative policies.

Given these pros and cons, it is not clear whether or not the coalition scheme is viable. Any conclusion would require in depth research.

Another possible way for a bank to provide information is to make precommitments regarding its asset management. For example, before it takes deposits, a bank may limit the scope of its investments to low risk assets such as government bonds, corporate bonds with minimum double A rating, and consumer loans. Such commitments would be a legal contract between the bank and its depositors. The bank invests only in the prescribed assets, and the depositors agree to accept a lower interest rate on the deposits. Depositors of this bank should not be alarmed by failures of some banks that have engaged in real estate ventures or speculated in stocks. This scheme is analogous to bond covenants of corporate bonds, which restrict the scope of the corporation's investment projects. Bond covenants can be a mutually beneficial arrangement. They enable a corporation to issue bonds at a low interest rate and at the same time satisfy risk-averse bond holders.

This section has briefly discussed possible schemes of providing information. Although providing information involves difficulties, it still appears possible. When a strong demand for bank-specific information arises, the market may find a better means than suggested in this section.

3. INCENTIVES TO PROVIDE INFORMATION

As described in the previous section, providing information
involves costly activities. Hence, banks will provide information
only when they have strong incentives to do so. The incentives
may be to prevent the contagion of bank failures and to attract
more depositors by proving the safety of banks.

The model has shown that competition motivates banks to
provide information. The U.S. had a relatively competitive banking
structure before the establishment of the Federal Reserve System.
Yet she experienced recurrent bank panics, indicating that there was
not enough information. This section considers possible
explanations for the lack of information.

To begin with, it is doubtful that banks would provide
information merely to prevent the contagion of bank failures. It
takes continuous efforts to keep the public informed of the financial
structure of a bank. In U.S. history, bank panics occurred with
intervals of ten to twenty years. Hence, it might have been cheaper
for banks to rely on collective efforts in dealing with bank panics.

Banks should have stronger incentives to provide information
when they can attract more depositors and increase profit by
providing information. This incentive should increase with
competition among banks. There may have been some factors in
U.S. history that discouraged the relatively competitive banks from
providing information.

Even in the 19th century, banking in the U.S. was far from
perfectly competitive. Banks may have enjoyed some geographical
monopoly power which was created by inhibited branch-banking
and limited transportation facilities.[5] With such monopoly power,
banks would be less pressed to provide financial information to
depositors. More importantly, banking was fairly standardized by
the National Bank Act of 1864. Important regulations imposed by
the act include minimum capital requirement (one hundred
thousand dollars), reserve requirements (25% for banks in the

central reserve cities and 15% for other banks), and maximum interest on loans (7%).[6] In a sense, these regulations served to prove the soundness of national banks relative to state banks. However, the standardized banking might have reduced depositors' incentives to monitor banks and hence banks' incentives to provide information individually. Consequently, banks might have become vulnerable to some exogenous shocks that were perceived to have undermined the solvency of the banking system as a whole. Furthermore, in the 19th century, the issuance of circulating notes was an important business of national banks. The notes were fully secured by government bonds deposited with the Treasury.[7] As a result, the note holders were not concerned about the credit-worthiness of a particular bank. This indifference of note holders along with the smaller segment of deposit banking might have reduced the importance of providing information to depositors.

Another possibility is that banks failed to find an effective, or cheap enough, means to provide information due to less advanced accounting and communication technologies. It appears that providing useful information was delayed in other sectors of the economy as well. For instance, the New York Stock Exchange was founded in 1792, but it was not until 1896 that the Dow Jones Industrial Average was introduced and not until 1923 that Standard and Poor's started rating corporate bonds.

In sum, a sufficient amount of bank-specific information was not available even when U.S. banking was relatively competitive. This information problem may be responsible for the recurrent bank panics in U.S. history. However, the existence of the information problem in banking history does not prove that the problem is not solvable.

NOTES

1. "In the case of professional and business 'clubs,' however, there can be a problem; if the club officials are to be drawn from the ranks of the competing, commercial members, there is the possibility of a conflict of interest." Goodhart, Charles. *The Evolution of Central Banks*, Cambridge: MIT Press, 1988, p.71.
2. In making the consumption arrangement of a good which is not either "purely private" or "purely Public," there generally exist both the optimal amount of the consumption and the optimal size of the "club" [consumption group]. Buchanan, James. "An Economic Theory of Club," *Economica*, 1965. The solvency information of banks would fall into the category of such goods. It has some "publicness", but the exclusion is possible.
3. Hirsch, Fred. "The Bagehot Problem," *The Manchester School of Economic and Social Studies*, 1977.
4. Comptroller of the Currency. *Annual Report*, Washington: U.S. Government Printing Office, 1907, p.66.
5. The National Bank Act practically prohibited national banks from having branches, and banking laws of most states also restricted branch banking. Fischer, Gerald. *American Banking Structure*, New York: Columbia University Press, 1968, p.19.
6. Bolles, Albert. *The National Bank Act and Its Judicial Meaning*, Philadelphia: George T. Bisel Co., 1910, pp.9, 225, 232.
7. Bolles, 1910, p.223.

CHAPTER VI

Conclusion

This study has identified the lack of bank-specific information as the main cause of bank panics. The model has shown how bank runs are disseminated when depositors maximize utility without information about the financial structure of individual banks. The main empirical findings are the following: The government or banks subdued bank panics mainly by providing the information that depositors lack; and bank runs were less contagious when depositors better understood the difference between problem banks and other solvent banks. These empirical findings confirm the crucial link between bank-specific information and bank panics.

Given these analyses, the bank panic is not a "mysterious" phenomenon caused by irrationality of the market, but an information problem that may be under the control of the market. It is true that banking involves a unique problem, namely, the problem of maintaining adequate liquidity. However, liquidity is not the major factor that inevitably invites bank runs and hence distinguishes banking from other businesses. The importance of solvency information shows that the market is primarily concerned about the solvency of banks. Banks' liquidity is a matter of secondary importance. Thus, banks should be able to protect themselves from bank failure contagion by maintaining solvency and informing their depositors of their solvency.

Identification of the nature and cause of bank panics enables us better to analyze the vulnerability of a banking system to runs and other issues surrounding bank panics. As shown by the model, a system with government provision of insurance enjoys enhanced public confidence and hence a reduced risk of bank runs. On the other hand, the insurance makes the public indifferent about the soundness of individual banks and hence reduces the availability of bank-specific information. When little bank-specific information is available, the government needs to commit extremely large resources to prevent bank runs. Thus, the cost of preventing bank runs can be very high. In a system free of government intervention, public confidence in the banking system as a whole would be lower. However, banks would have strong incentives to provide their financial information. Depositors having bank-specific information would not run on solvent banks. Thus, information, to some extent, can compensate for lower systemwide confidence.

In conclusion, though the contagion of bank failures differentiates banking from other businesses and complicates banking matters, the difference is not fundamental. Therefore, the possibility of bank failure contagion neither implies that competitive banking is inherently unstable, nor does it by itself justify excessive intervention of the government.

Tables

Table 1
Causes of Bank Failures in the 19th Century[a]

Cause	Number of Failures
Defalcation of officers	3
Defalcation of officers and fraudulent management	23
Defalcation of officers and excessive loans to others	1
Defalcation of officers and depreciation of securities	2
Depreciation of securities	5

Excessive loans to others, injudicious banking, and depreciation of securities	13
Excessive loans to officers and directors and depreciation of securities	12
Excessive loans to officers and directors and investments in real estate and mortgages	6
Excessive loans to others and depreciation of securities	1
Excessive loans to others and investments in real estate and mortgages	3
Excessive loans and failure of large debtors	1
Excessive loans to officers and directors	3
Failure of large debtors	4
Fraudulent management	7
Fraudulent management, excessive loans to officers and directors, and depreciation of securities	14
Fraudulent management and depreciation of securities	12
Fraudulent management and injudicious banking	18

Fraudulent management, defalcation of officers, and depreciation of securities	7
Fraudulent management, injudicious banking, investments in real estate and mortgages, and depreciation of securities	5
Fraudulent management, excessive loans to officers and directors, and excessive loans to others	9
Injudicious banking	14
Injudicious banking and depreciation of securities	40
Injudicious banking and failure of large debtors	8
Investments in real estate and mortgages and depreciation of securities	9
General stringency of money market, shrinkage in value, and imprudent methods of banking	24
Unreported	2
TOTAL	246

[a]National banks placed in the hands receivers in the years between 1865 and 1893.

Source: Comptroller of the Currency, 1893, pp.180-191.

Table 2

Financial Condition of Banks in September, 1873[a]

Date[b]	Deposits	Legal tenders	Specie	Reserve[c] Percentage
Sep. 1	$220,390,300	$44,729,300	$23,095,200	27.15%
Sep. 6	$212,772,700	$38,679,900	$21,767,000	24.95%
Sep. 13	$207,317,500	$36,717,200	$20,442,300	23.89%
Sep. 20	$198,040,100	$34,307,900	$18,884,600	23.03%
Sep. 26	$174,527,800	$21,229,100	$12,937,300	16.97%

[a]Aggregate of member banks of the New York Clearing House Association.

[b]Until September 20, the member banks issued their financial statements through the clearing house on a weekly basis. However, owing to the financial crisis, they stopped reporting and did not resume the regular reporting until November. Sprague collected the data of September 26 from contemporary newspapers. As to the accuracy of the data, there is some room for questions. However, we may very well infer the financial difficulties experienced by banks from the fact that they stopped reporting.

[c](legal tenders + Specie)/(deposits + bank notes outstanding) × 100

Sources: Sprague (1910, p.52); Comptroller of the Currency (1873, p.24); *Banker's Magazine* (1873, p.325).

Table 3

Financial Condition of Banks in October and November, 1873[a]

Date[b]	Deposits	Legal Tenders	Specie
Oct. 13	89,664,948	6,517,250	10,031,407
Nov. 1	92,563,997	15,668,452	11,499,457
Nov. 22	138,625,300	25,330,600	14,759,300

[a]Aggregate of national banks in New York City. The Comptroller of the Currency obtained these data by issuing a circular requesting all national banks to report their financial conditions on October 13 and November 1. Thus, this table should not be viewed as a continuation of Table 2 which shows the financial condition of the clearing-house member banks.

[b]According to the Comptroller of the Currency, New York banks held the smallest amount of legal tender notes on Oct. 13.

Source: Comptroller of the Currency (1873, p.31).

Table 4

Licensing of Bank Reopening after the Suspension of 1933

Type of banks[b]	Number of licensed banks	Number of unlicensed banks[a]
As of March 15, 1933		
National banks	4,507	1,400
State member banks	571	221
Nonmember banks	NA	NA[c]
As of March 29, 1933		
National banks	4,766	NA
State member banks	621	NA
Nonmember Banks	NA	NA

As of April 12, 1933		
National banks	4,789	1,108
State member banks	636	148
Nonmember banks	7,392	2,959
As of January 1, 1934		
National banks	NA	452
State member banks	NA	60
Nonmember Banks	NA	1,257

[a]Unlicensed banks do not include banks placed in liquidation or receivership.

[b]Member banks mean the members of the Federal Reserve System. The membership was required for national banks and optional for state banks.

[c]Data are not available.

Sources: Federal Reserve Board (1933a, p.64), Federal Reserve Board (1933b, p.216), Upham and Lamke (1934, p.47).

Table 5
Economic Condition in 1880's

Year	Production Index[a]	Price Index[b]
1880	27.0	82
1881	27.4	85
1882	30.9	87
1883	30.6	84
1884	30.8	79
1885	29.7	77
1886	35.2	76
1887	36.6	77
1888	37.3	78
1889	41.5	77

[a]A weighted average of a number of leading manufactured commodities.

[b]1913 = 100.

Source: U.S. Department of Commerce (1949, pp.179, 186, 187).

Table 6
Financial Condition of New York Banks in 1884

Date	Specie	Legal Tenders	Deposits	Surplus
Apr. 5	61,950,200	28,246,000	343,969,300	4,203,874
Apr. 12	63,864,200	25,840,400	344,352,300	3,616,425
Apr. 19	60,750,400	26,981,500	340,661,300	2,566,575
Apr. 26	58,215,300	28,125,500	335,684,000	2,419,800
May 3	55,997,100	28,112,800	333,215,600	806,000
May 10	58,841,700	28,069,300	329,822,200	4,455,450
May 17	56,314,100	26,113,100	317,200,700	3,127,025
May 24	45,510,000	22,026,700	296,575,300	6,607,125
May 31	45,985,600	24,129,100	288,361,100	1,975,625
June 7	46,187,600	25,984,700	283,323,200	1,341,500
June 14	48,687,400	28,577,000	281,111,600	6,986,500
June 21	51,348,600	28,846,000	280,698,100	10,025,075
June 28	55,817,900	28,813,000	286,158,300	13,126,625
July 5	60,851,800	28,027,000	290,304,000	16,302,800
July 12	68,612,600	30,128,400	299,552,000	23,853,000
July 19	72,731,600	31,873,700	304,788,100	28,408,279
July 26	74,792,788	32,229,800	305,577,500	30,628,125

Source: *Bankers' Magazine* (1884).

Table 7
Flows of Currency and Gold to New York Banks[a]
(In thousands of dollars)

Date Week Ending	Currency			Gold			Total
	In	Out	Gain	In	Out	Gain	Gain[b]
Feb.29	1,082	813	269	120	237	(117)	152
Mar. 7	728	683	45	120	150	(30)	15
Mar.14	647	914	(267)	–	426	(426)	(693)
Mar.21	640	1,015	(375)	–	300	(300)	(675)
Mar.28	701	1,500	(799)	15	–	15	(784)
Apr. 4	948	1,969	(1,021)	–	300	(300)	(1,321)
Apr.11	1,722	278	1,444	30	282	(252)	1,192
Apr.18	2,093	362	1,731	245	414	(169)	1,562
Apr.25	3,150	254	2,896	50	–	50	2,946
May 2	3,426	356	3,070	60	–	60	3,130
May 9	4,300	503	3,797	–	–	–	3,797

May 16	2,498	1,825	673	—	1,780	(1,780)	(1,107)
May 23	1,242	2,278	(1,036)	50	1,340	(1,290)	(2,326)
May 30	2,038	462	1,576	30	680	(650)	926
June 6	2,540	1,346	1,194	35	700	(665)	529
June 13	3,008	735	2,273	0	420	(420)	1,853

[a]Flows caused by movements to and from the interior.

[b]Numbers in parenthesis are losses.

Source: *Commercial and Financial Chronicle* (1884).

Table 8
Activities in the New York Stock Exchange

Year	Index of Common Stock Prices[a]			Sales Volume (in Millions)		Sale of Membership	
	All	Railroad	Industrial	No. of Shares	Value	Highest	Lowest
1878	26.7	30.7	17.0	40	2,157	9,500	4,250
1879	32.6	38.1	18.1	73	4,137	16,000	5,100
1880	41.2	49.3	20.1	98	6,819	26,000	14,000
1881	49.5	59.4	23.6	115	8,198	30,000	22,000
1882	46.7	55.7	28.4	116	7,689	32,500	20,000
1883	44.5	53.5	21.9	97	6,261	30,000	23,000
1884	37.4	45.0	19.9	96	5,940	27,000	20,000
1885	36.3	43.4	21.3	93	5,480	34,000	20,000
1886	42.4	50.8	24.1	101	5,886	33,000	23,000
1887	43.7	52.4	25.2	85	4,509	30,000	19,000

[a]1926 = 100.

Sources: U.S. Department of Commerce (1949, pp.280, 282); Eames (1894, pp.85, 95).

Table 9
Banking Panics in the United States

YEAR: 1837

Economic Environments: Land and cotton boom in the 1830's.

Proximate Cause: Collapse of the cotton business.

Major Events:
  Mar. 14 --- Bankruptcy of cotton houses in New Orleans
  May 10 --- New York banks suspended specie payments.

Bank Failures:
  Number of banks failed - 618[a]
  Total number of banks - 788

Sources: Lightner (1922, pp.126, 127) and Collman (1931,
         pp.59-65).

YEAR: 1857

Economic Environments: Railroad boom; Speculation in the stock
                       market in the 1850's.

Proximate Cause: Stock market crash caused by failures of
                 railroad companies.

Major Events:

Aug. 20 --- Failure of the Ohio Life Insurance & Trust Company which had made imprudent advances to Western Railroads. The stock of Western Railroads was substantially overvalued, and the failure became a major disturbance in the stock market.

September --- Runs on the Metropolitan Bank and the Bank of Commerce.

Oct. 15 --- Banks in New York City suspended specie payments.

Sources: Sobel (1968, pp.99-106) and Collman (1931, pp.83-88).

YEAR: 1873

Economic Environments: Railroad boom; Four years of rapid economic growth.

Proximate Cause: Excessive loan expansion to railroad companies and decline of the railroad business.

Major Events:

Sep. 8 --- Suspension of the New York Warehouse and Security Company which was financially involved with the Missouri, Kansas, and Texas Railroad.

Sep. 13 --- Failure of Messrs Kenyon, Cox & Co. that endorsed Canada Southern Railway paper.

Sep. 18 --- Major bank runs started.

Sep. 20 --- Closing of New York Stock Exchange.

Sep. 24 --- Suspension of currency payments by New York banks.

Bank Failures:
    Number of bank suspensions - 37[b]
    Total number of banks - 1968
    Average number of bank suspensions
    in the previous five years - 9

Sources: *Commercial and Financial Chronicle* (1873, p.382),
        Comptroller of the Currency (1873, pp.26-31), and
        Sprague (1910, pp.153-180).

YEAR: 1884

Economic Environments: Moderate economic downturn; Decline of
                        the general price level.

Proximate Cause: Disclosure of fraud and embezzlement.

Major Events:
    May 6 --- Failure of the Marine National Bank that was
              financially connected with an insolvent brokerage
              firm, Grant & Ward.
    May 8 --- Failure of Grant & Ward that committed a major
              fraud.
    May 13 --- Disclosure of an embezzlement by the president of
              the Second National Bank.
    May 14 --- Runs on New York banks.
              Authorization of Clearing house loan certificates.

Bank Failures:
    Number of bank suspensions - 60
    Total number of banks - 4113
    Average number of bank suspensions
    in the previous five years - 20

Source: Comptroller of the Currency (1884, pp.33, 34).

YEAR: 1893

Economic Environments: Monetary disturbance caused by Sherman Silver Purchase Act and international gold flows.

Proximate Cause: Stock market collapse in May.

Major Events:
Feb. 26 --- The failure of the Philadelphia and Reading Railroad.
May 4 --- The failure of the National Cordage Company (Trust Company) which caused the stock market collapse.
July --- Numerous bank failures throughout the nation. Reserve outflows from New York banks.
Aug. 5 --- Suspension of payments by New York banks.

Bank Failures:
Number of bank suspensions - 491
Total number of banks - 9492
Average number of bank suspensions
in the previous five years - 47

Sources: Sprague (1910, pp.153-180) and Sobel (1968, pp.251-255).

YEAR: 1907

Economic Environments: A steady rise in price level and an economic boom in 1900's.

Proximate Cause: Failure of an attempt to corner copper stocks.

Major Events:
Oct. 17 --- Run on the Mercantile National Bank that attempted to corner the stock of the United Copper Company.
Oct. 21 --- Runs on Knickerbocker Trust Company that was financially involved with the Mercantile National Bank.
Major bank runs started.
Oct. 22 --- Suspension of Knickerbocker Trust Company.
Oct. 23 --- Major runs on trust companies.

Bank Failures:
Number of bank suspensions - 122[c]
Total number of banks - 19746
Average number of bank suspensions in the previous five years - 73

Sources: Comptroller of the Currency (1907, p.70) and Sprague (pp.246-260).

YEAR: 1933

Economic Environments: An economic depression following the speculative boom of the 1920's.

Proximate Cause: Stock market crash in 1929.

Major Events:
  Dec. 11, 1930 --- The Bank of United States in New York City
            was closed.
  1930 - 1933 --- Large number of bank failures and sustained
            deposit outflows.
  Oct. 31, 1932 --- Statewide bank suspension in Nevada.
  Feb. 14, 1933 --- Statewide bank suspension in Michigan.
  Mar. 6, 1933 --- Nationwide bank suspension.

Bank Failures:
  Number of bank suspensions - 4004
  Total number of banks - 14624
  Average number of bank suspensions
  in the previous five years - 1252

Sources: Upham and Lamke (1934, pp.6-16) and Kennedy (1973).

[a]This figure is from Lightner (1922). All other figures about the number of bank failures or suspensions are from U.S. Department of Commerce (1949).

[b]Temporary suspensions are included, but suspensions under the declaration of special banking holidays are not included.

[c]Average of years 1907 and 1908. The panic spanned from the end of 1907 to the beginning of 1908.

Table 10

Money Supply at the Beginning of 1890's

(in millions of dollars)

Year	Treasury Notes of 1990	Other U.S. Notes	Total U.S. Notes	Net Gold Exports
1890	0	334.689	334.689	4.331
1891	40.349	343.207	383.556	68.130
1892	98.259	339.400	437.657	0.496
1893	140.856	330.774	471.630	87.507

Source: U.S. Bureau of Census (1949, pp.244, 275).

Table 11
Bank Suspensions in 1893

Month	Number of Suspensions	Region	Number of Suspensions
January	2	Northeast	5
February	2	South	52
March	2	Midwest	55
April	2	West	45
May	13	Territories	1
June	25		
July	74		
August	32		
September	1		
October	5		
Total	158		158

Source: Comptroller of the Currency (1893, pp.75-80).

Table 12
Daily Stock Price before
the Failure of the Marine National Bank on May 6, 1884

Date	Stock Price Index[a]
Apr.28 (Mon.)	100.0000
Apr.29 (Tue.)	99.2284
Apr.30 (Wed.)	99.0229
May 1 (Thur.)	99.8674
May 2 (Fri.)	99.5100
May 3 (Sat.)	99.7925
May 5 (Mon.)	100.3705
May 6 (Tue.)	100.1206

[a]The index has been calculated based on the prices of 85 stocks regularly listed by the *Banker's Magazine* (1884, pp.893-895, 977-979). All stocks have been equally weighted.

Table 13
Major Banks Involved in Financial Crises

The panic of 1873

National Bank of Commonwealth
Date of Suspension: Sep. 20

Capital	Loans and Discounts	Deposits
750,000	1,951,900	1,803,800

As of Aug. 18, 1873.

The Panic of 1884

Marine National Bank
Date of Suspension: May 6

Capital	Loans and Discounts	Deposits
400,000	4,451,000	5,134,000

Metropolitan National Bank
Date of Suspension: May 14

Capital	Loans and Discounts	Deposits
3,000,000	11,239,000	8,857,800

As of Apr. 19, 1884.

The Panic of 1893

National German-American Bank, St. Paul, Minn.[a]
Date of Suspension: Aug. 4

Capital	Loans and Discounts	Deposits
2,000,000	NA	NA[b]

National Bank of Deposit[c]
Date of Suspension: May 22

Capital	Loans and Discounts	Deposits
300,000	NA	NA

The Panic of 1907

Mercantile National Bank

Capital	Loans and Discounts	Deposits
3,000,000	NA	16,014,900

National Bank of North America

Capital	Loans and Discounts	Deposits
2,000,000	NA	16,759,800

As of Mar. 22, 1873.

[a]The bank with the largest capital suspended in 1893.

[b]Data are not available.

[c]The only bank located in the New York City suspended in 1893.

Sources: *Commercial and Financial Chronicle* and Comptroller
of the Currency.

Table 14
Major Institutional Developments of U.S. Banking

1781 - The establishment of the Bank of North America.
Significance: The first federally chartered bank; the bank
is commonly regarded as the first modern style bank of the
U.S.

1791 - The incorporation of the First Bank of the United States.[a]
Significance: Government participation in the bank capital
(one fifth); the bank's involvement in the government
finance.

1818 - The incorporation of the Second Bank of the United States.[b]
Significance: Similar to the first bank of the United States.

1838 - The passage of Free Banking Act in New York.
Significance: Removal of political discretion in bank
chartering, which had served as a major entry barrier.
Under the act, individuals or associations were permitted to
engage in banking if they met a set of prescribed conditions.
The movement was followed by many other states, and the
act became a basis of U.S. banking laws.

1863 - The establishment of the Office of the Comptroller of the
currency.
Significance: More Systematic and uniform treatments of
banking matters.

1864 - The enactment of the National Bank Act.
Significance: The establishment of the National Banking System under uniform standards.

1913 - The enactment of the Federal Reserve Act.
Significance: The establishment of Federal Reserve System; significant enhancement of the government's ability to control money stocks.

1933 - The enactment of the Banking Act of 1933.
Significance: The establishment of the Federal Deposit Insurance Corporation; tighter banking regulations including the interest rate ceilings on deposits and a limited scope of banks' asset holdings.

1980 - The enactment of the Depository Institutions Deregulation Act.
Significance: the act was followed by deregulatory movements such as the phase-out of Regulation Q (interest on deposits).

[a]The charter was expired in 1811 and was not renewed.

[b]The charter was not renewed, and the bank obtained the charter from the state of Pennsylvania in 1936, ending the relationship with the federal government.

Graphs

1. Deposits Held by Individuals

Graphs 1.a-1.d show the behavior of deposits at national banks held by individuals. Deposits held by individuals may best reflect public confidence in the banking system.

Dates of observation are:

For 1872 - 1874;
    Feb. 27, Apr. 19, June 10, Oct. 3, Dec. 27, 1872
    Feb. 28, Apr. 25, June 13, Sep. 12, Dec. 26, 1873
    Feb. 27, May 1, June 26, Oct. 2, Dec. 31, 1874

For 1883 - 1885;
    Mar. 13, May 1, June 22, Oct. 2, Dec. 31, 1883
    Mar. 7, Apr. 24, June 20, Sep. 30, Dec. 20, 1884
    Mar. 10, May 6, July 1, Oct. 1, Dec. 24, 1885

For 1892 - 1894;
   Mar. 1, May 17, July 12, Sep. 30, Dec. 9, 1892
   Mar. 6, May 4, July 12, Oct. 3, Dec. 19, 1893
   Feb. 28, May 4, July 18, Oct. 2, Dec. 19, 1894
For 1906 - 1907;
   Jan. 29, Apr. 6, June 18, Sep. 4, Nov. 12, 1906
   Jan. 26, Mar. 22, May 20, Aug. 22, Dec. 3, 1907
   Feb. 14, May 14, July 15, Sep. 23, 1908

Note: The arrow on the graphs indicates the culmination
      time of the panic (Refer to Table 9).

Data Source: Comptroller of the Currency (1908, pp.492-523).

2. Deposits Held by Individuals II

Graphs 2.a-2.d adjusts Graphs 1.a-1.d for the time trend. These
figures are the residuals of OLS estimation using the deposits as
the dependent variable and time as the independent variable.

Regression Output

Constant	595.1
X Coefficient	104.6
Standard Error	2.51
R Squared	0.889
No. of Observations	219
Degrees of Freedom	217

3. The Ratio of Currency to Deposits

Graphs 3.a-3.d show the quarterly averages of the currency deposit ratio.

Data Source: Friedman and Schwartz (1963, pp.61-69).

4. The Ratio of Capital to Risky Assets

The risky assets include loans and discounts and securities held by banks other than government bonds. These figures are the aggregate amounts of the capital of national banks divided by the aggregate amount of their risky assets.

Dates of observation are:

For 1871 - 1874;
  Apr. 29, June 10, Oct. 2, Dec. 16, 1971
  Feb. 27, Apr. 19, June 10, Oct. 3, Dec. 27, 1872
  Feb. 28, Apr. 25, June 13, Sep. 12, Dec. 26, 1873
  Feb. 27, 1874

For 1882 - 1885;
  May 19, July 1, Oct. 3, Dec. 30, 1882
  Mar. 13, May 1, June 22, Oct. 2, Dec. 31, 1883
  Mar. 7, Apr. 24, June 20, Sep. 30, Dec. 20, 1884
  Mar. 10, 1885

For 1891 - 1894;
  July 9, Sep. 25, Dec. 2, 1891
  Mar. 1, May 17, July 12, Sep. 30, Dec. 9, 1892
  Mar. 6, May 4, July 12, Oct. 3, Dec. 19, 1893
  Feb. 28, May 4, 1894

For 1905 - 1907;
   May. 29, Aug. 25, Nov. 9, 1905
   Jan. 29, Apr. 6, June 18, Sep. 4, Nov. 12, 1906
   Jan. 26, Mar. 22, May 20, Aug. 22, Dec. 3, 1907
   Feb. 14, May 14, 1908

Note: The arrow on the graphs indicates the date of observation
   immediately preceding the panic.

Data Source: Comptroller of the Currency (1908, pp.492-523).

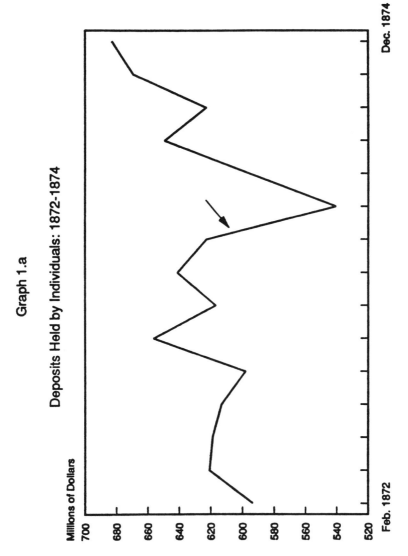

Graph 1.a

Deposits Held by Individuals: 1872-1874

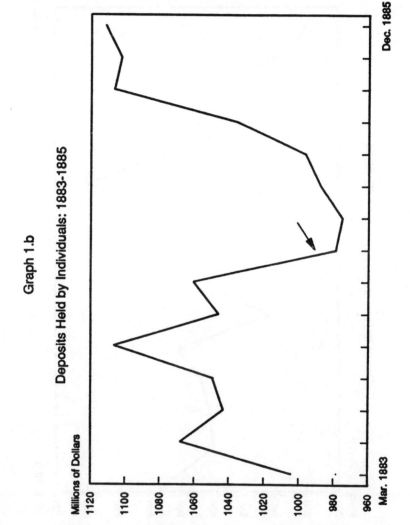

Graph 1.b

Deposits Held by Individuals: 1883-1885

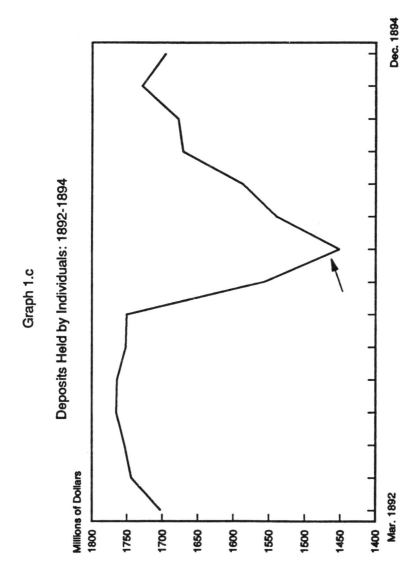

Graph 1.c

Deposits Held by Individuals: 1892-1894

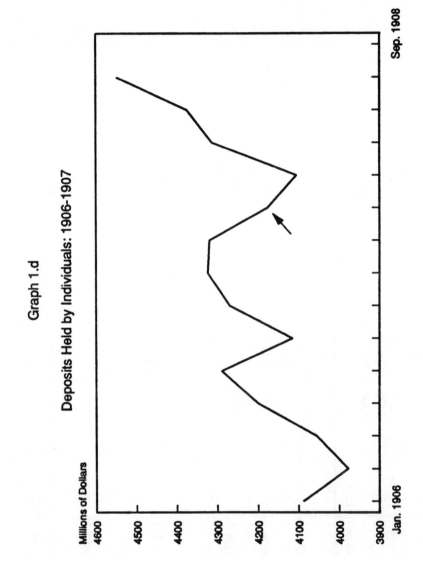

Graph 1.d

Deposits Held by Individuals: 1906-1907

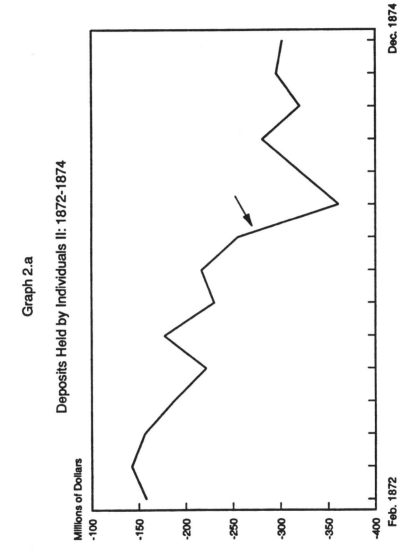

Graph 2.a

Deposits Held by Individuals II: 1872-1874

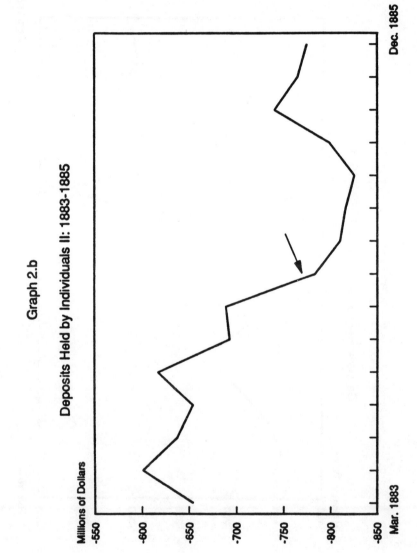

Graph 2.b

Deposits Held by Individuals II: 1883-1885

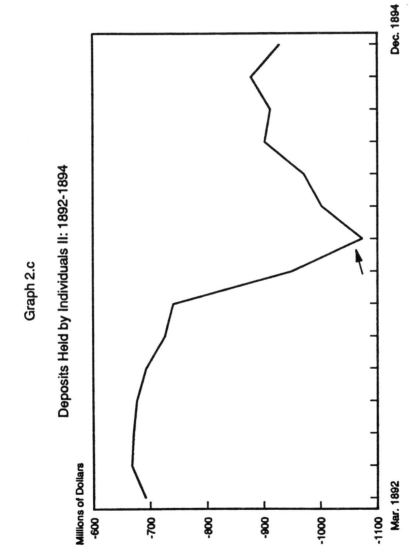

Graph 2.c

Deposits Held by Individuals II: 1892-1894

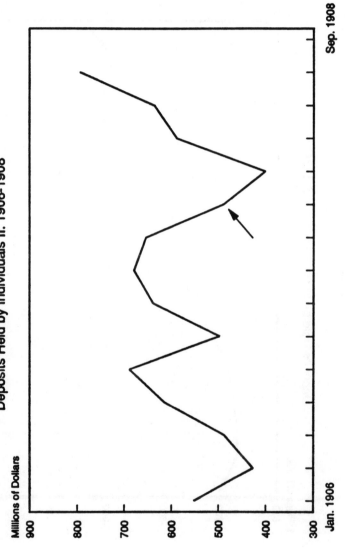

Graph 2.d

Deposits Held by Individuals II: 1906-1908

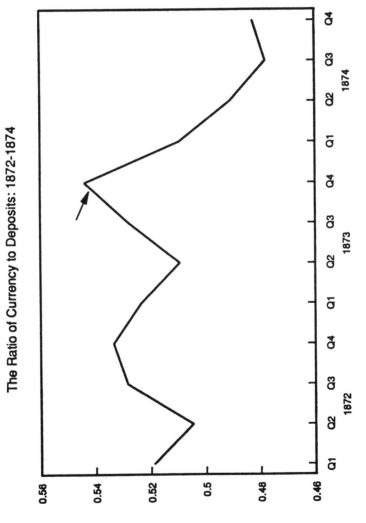

Graph 3.a

The Ratio of Currency to Deposits: 1872-1874

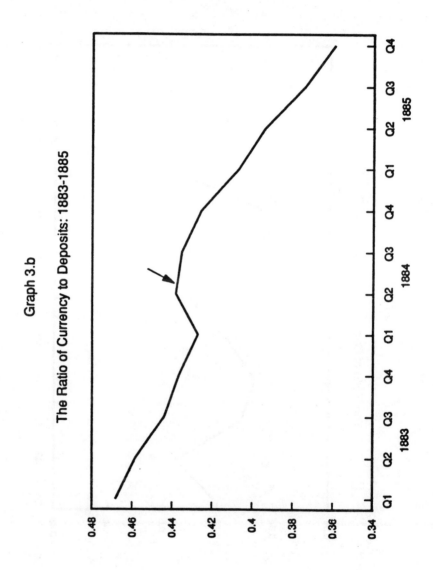

Graph 3.b

The Ratio of Currency to Deposits: 1883-1885

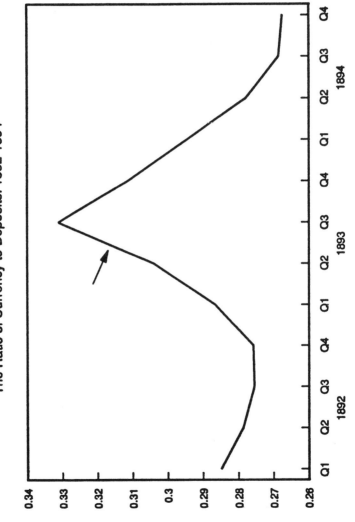

Graph 3.c

The Ratio of Currency to Deposits: 1892-1894

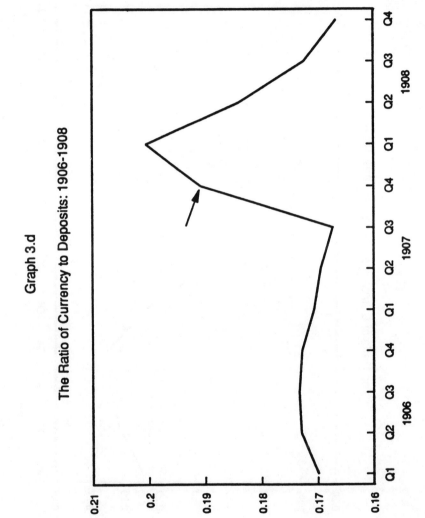

Graph 3.d

The Ratio of Currency to Deposits: 1906-1908

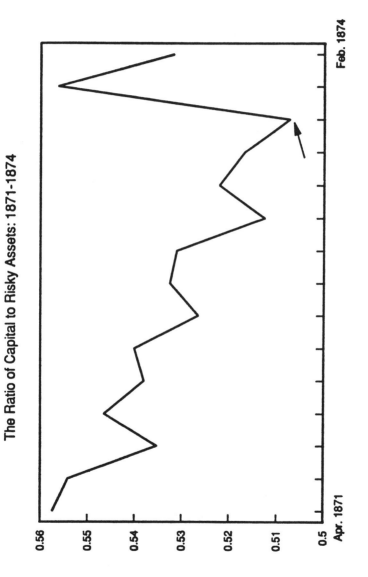

Graph 4.a

The Ratio of Capital to Risky Assets: 1871-1874

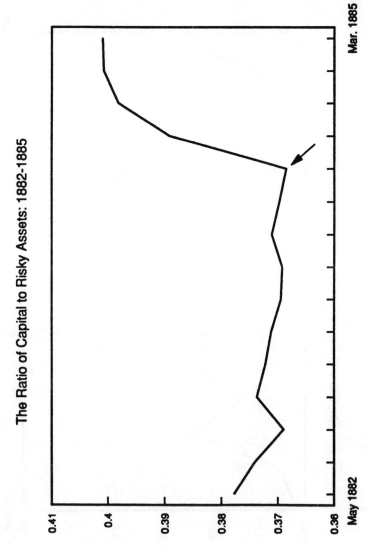

Graph 4.b

The Ratio of Capital to Risky Assets: 1882-1885

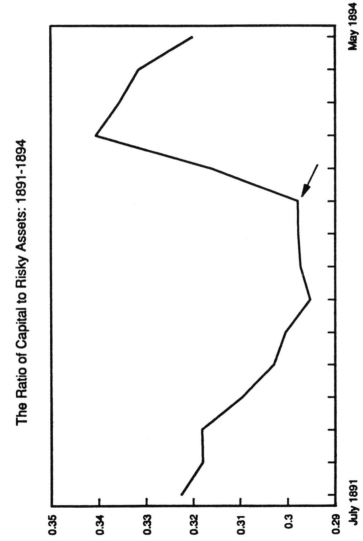

Graph 4.c

The Ratio of Capital to Risky Assets: 1891-1894

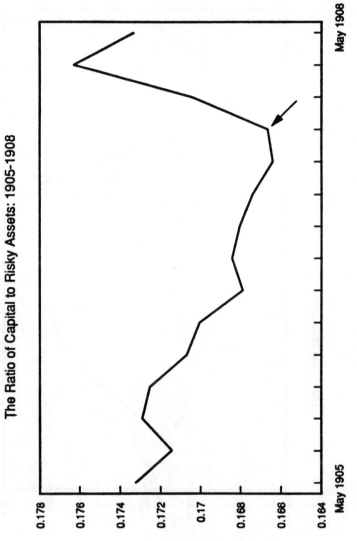

Graph 4.d

The Ratio of Capital to Risky Assets: 1905-1908

Appendices

Appendix 1

By C3, the distribution of type A bank is independent to that of type B, and:

$$n_A \sim b(N_A, p_A) \quad \text{and} \quad n_B \sim b(N_B, p_B)$$

To facilitate algebraic manipulation, these binimial random variables are approximated as Poisson random variables. Then,

$$h(n_A) = \exp. \{-N_A \cdot p_A\} \frac{(N_A \cdot p_A)^{n_A}}{n_A!}$$

$$h(n_B) = \exp. \{-N_B \cdot p_B\} \frac{(N_B \cdot p_B)^{n_B}}{n_B!}$$

where h denotes probability density function.

By independence, the density of random variable, $n = n_A + n_B$:

$$h(n) - \exp.\{ -(N_A \cdot p_A + N_B \cdot p_B) \}$$

$$\times \frac{(N_A \cdot p_A + N_B \cdot p_B)^n}{n!}$$

Using the definitions, $N_A + N_B = N$ and $N_B / N = \theta$,

$$h(n) - \exp.\{ -N \cdot p_A - \theta \cdot N \cdot (p_B - p_A) \}$$

$$\times \frac{\{ N \cdot p_A + \theta \cdot N \cdot (p_B - p_A) \}^n}{n!}$$

$$E(N) - N \cdot p_A + \theta \cdot N \cdot (p_B - p_A)$$

Given this result, $h(n \mid \theta_1) = h(n \mid \theta_2)$ when:

$$\exp.\{ -N \cdot p_A - \theta_1 \cdot N \cdot (p_B - p_A) \}$$

$$\times \frac{\{ N \cdot p_A + \theta_1 \cdot N \cdot (p_B - p_A) \}^n}{n!}$$

$$- \exp.\{ -N \cdot p_A - \theta_2 \cdot N \cdot (p_B - p_A) \}$$

$$\times \frac{\{ N \cdot p_A + \theta_2 \cdot N \cdot (p_B - p_A) \}^n}{n!}$$

Taking natural log on both sides,

$$-N\bar{p}_A - \theta_1 \cdot N \cdot (p_B - p_A) + n \cdot \ln\{N\bar{p}_A + \theta_1 \cdot N \cdot (p_B - p_A)\} - \ln(n!)$$

$$= -N\bar{p}_A - \theta_2 \cdot N \cdot (p_B - p_A) + n \cdot \ln\{N\bar{p}_A + \theta_2 \cdot N \cdot (p_B - p_A)\} - \ln(n!)$$

By cancelling and rearranging terms,

$$N \cdot (p_B - p_A) \cdot (\theta_2 - \theta_1)$$

$$= n \cdot \ln\left\{\frac{p_A + \theta_2 \cdot (p_B - p_A)}{p_A + \theta_1 \cdot (p_B - p_A)}\right\}$$

Hence,

$$n^* = \frac{N \cdot (p_B - p_A) \cdot (\theta_2 - \theta_1)}{\ln\left\{\dfrac{p_A + \theta_2 \cdot (p_B - p_A)}{p_A + \theta_1 \cdot (p_B - p_A)}\right\}}$$

Appendix 2

From appendix I,

$$h(n) = \exp.\{ -N \cdot p_A - \theta \cdot N \cdot (p_B - p_A) \}$$

$$\times \frac{\{N \cdot p_A + \theta \cdot N \cdot (p_B - p_A)\}^n}{n!}$$

The first difference with respect to n is:

$$\frac{\Delta h}{\Delta n} = h(n) - h(n-1)$$

$$= \exp.\{ -N \cdot p_A - \theta \cdot N \cdot (p_B - p_A) \}$$

$$\times \frac{\{N \cdot p_A + \theta \cdot N \cdot (p_B - p_A)\}^n}{n!}$$

$$- \exp.\{ -N \cdot p_A - \theta \cdot N \cdot (p_B - p_A) \}$$

$$\times \frac{\{N \cdot p_A + \theta \cdot N \cdot (p_B - p_A)\}^{n-1}}{(n-1)!}$$

$$- \exp.\{ -N \cdot p_A - \theta \cdot N \cdot (p_B - p_A) \}$$

$$\times \ \frac{\{ N \cdot p_A + \theta \cdot N \cdot (p_B - p_A) \}^{n-1}}{(n-1)!}$$

$$\times \ \left\{ \frac{N \cdot p_A + \theta \cdot N \cdot (p_B - p_A)}{n} - 1 \right\}$$

The first two terms of the above expression are unambiguously positive. Hence,

$$\frac{\Delta h}{\Delta n} > 0 \qquad when \quad n < N \cdot p_A + \theta \cdot N \cdot (p_B - p_A)$$

$$\frac{\Delta h}{\Delta n} - 0 \qquad when \quad n - N \cdot p_A + \theta \cdot N \cdot (p_B - p_A)$$

$$\frac{\Delta h}{\Delta n} < 0 \qquad when \quad n > N \cdot p_A + \theta \cdot N \cdot (p_B - p_A)$$

From appendix 1, $E(n \mid \theta_i) = N p_A + \theta_i \cdot N \cdot (p_B - p_A)$. Given this result, $h(n \mid \theta_1)$ is maximized when $E(n \mid \theta_1)$, and $h(n \mid \theta_2)$ is maximized when $E(n \mid \theta_2)$. In addition, $h(\theta \mid n)$ is maximized when $\theta = (n - N p_A) / N \cdot (p_B - p_A)$. That is, the largest likelihood function for a given n is the one whose expected number equals n.

Let $n = E(n \mid \theta_i) = N \overline{p}_A + \theta_i \cdot N \cdot (p_B - p_A)$, and

$$w = N \overline{p}_A + \theta \cdot N \cdot (p_B - p_A).$$

Then

$$h(n \mid \theta) - \exp.\{-w\} \; \frac{w^n}{n!}$$

$$\frac{\partial h}{\partial \theta} - -\theta \cdot N \cdot (p_B - p_A) \cdot \exp.\{-w\} \; \frac{w^n}{n!}$$

$$+ \; \theta \cdot N \cdot (p_B - p_A) \cdot n \cdot \exp.\{-w\} \; \frac{w^{n-1}}{n!}$$

$$- \; \theta \cdot N \cdot (p_B - p_A) \cdot \exp.\{-w\} \; \frac{w^{n-1}}{n!} \cdot (n - w)$$

$$- \; \theta \cdot N \cdot (p_B - p_A) \cdot \exp.\{-w\} \; \frac{w^{n-1}}{n!}$$

$$\times \; [\{N \cdot p_A + \theta_i \cdot N \cdot (p_B - P_A)\}$$

$$- \{N \cdot p_A + \theta \cdot N \cdot (p_B - p_A)\}]$$

$$- \theta \cdot N \cdot (p_B - p_A) \cdot \exp.\{-w\} \frac{w^{n-1}}{n!}$$

$$\times [N \cdot (p_B - P_A) \cdot (\theta_i - \theta)]$$

Hence, $h(\theta \mid n)$ is maximized when θ equals θ_i. Given this result,

$L(n \mid \theta_1) > L(n \mid \theta_2)$ when $n = E(n \mid \theta_1)$, and

$L(n \mid \theta_1) < L(n \mid \theta_2)$ when $n = E(n \mid \theta_2)$.

Therefore,

$$N p_A + \theta_1 \cdot N \cdot (p_B - p_A) < n^* < N p_A + \theta_2 \cdot N \cdot (p_B - p_A)$$

and

$L(n \mid \theta_1) > L(n \mid \theta_2)$ if $n < n^*$

$L(n \mid \theta_1) = L(n \mid \theta_2)$ if $n = n^*$

$L(n \mid \theta_1) < L(n \mid \theta_2)$ if $n > n^*$

Appendix 3

Let

$$Z = \frac{L(n \mid \theta_1)}{L(n \mid \theta_2)}$$

Then,

$$\frac{\Delta Z}{\Delta n} = Z(n) - Z(n-1)$$

$$= [\exp.\{ -N \cdot p_A - \theta_1 \cdot N \cdot (p_B - p_A) \}$$

$$\times \frac{\{N \cdot p_A + \theta_1 \cdot N \cdot (p_B - p_A) \}^n}{n!} \Bigg] \Bigg/$$

$$[\exp.\{ -N \cdot p_A - \theta_2 \cdot N \cdot (p_B - p_A) \}$$

$$\times \frac{\{N \cdot p_A + \theta_2 \cdot N \cdot (p_B - p_A) \}^n}{n!} \Bigg]$$

$$- \left[\exp. \{ -N \cdot p_A - \theta_1 \cdot N \cdot (p_B - p_A) \} \right.$$

$$\times \left. \frac{\{ N \cdot p_A + \theta_1 \cdot N \cdot (p_B - p_A) \}^{n-1}}{(n-1)!} \right] \Bigg/$$

$$\left[\exp. \{ -N \cdot p_A - \theta_2 \cdot N \cdot (p_B - p_A) \} \right.$$

$$\times \left. \frac{\{ N \cdot p_A + \theta_2 \cdot N \cdot (p_B - p_A) \}^{n-1}}{(n-1)!} \right]$$

$$- \left[\exp. \{ -N \cdot p_A - \theta_1 \cdot N \cdot (p_B - p_A) \} \right.$$

$$\times \frac{\{ N \cdot p_A + \theta_1 \cdot N \cdot (p_B - p_A) \}^{n}}{n!}$$

$$- \exp. \{ -N \cdot p_A - \theta_1 \cdot N \cdot (p_B - p_A) \}$$

$$\times \frac{\{ N \cdot p_A + \theta_1 \cdot N \cdot (p_B - p_A) \}^{n-1}}{(n-1)!}$$

$$\times \left. \frac{\{ N \cdot p_A + \theta_2 \cdot N \cdot (p_B - p_A) \}}{n} \right] \Bigg/$$

$$[\exp.\{ -N \cdot p_A - \theta_2 \cdot N \cdot (p_B - p_A)\}$$

$$\times \frac{\{N \cdot p_A + \theta_2 \cdot N \cdot (p_B - p_A)\}^n}{n!}]$$

$$- [\exp.\{ -N \cdot p_A - \theta_1 \cdot N \cdot (p_B - p_A)\}$$

$$\times \frac{\{N \cdot p_A + \theta_1 \cdot N \cdot (p_B - p_A)\}^{n-1}}{n!}$$

$$\times \{N \cdot (p_B - p_A) \cdot (\theta_1 - \theta_2)\}] \ /$$

$$[\exp.\{ -N \cdot p_A - \theta_2 \cdot N \cdot (p_B - p_A)\}$$

$$\times \frac{\{N \cdot p_A + \theta_2 \cdot N \cdot (p_B - p_A)\}^n}{n!}]$$

Since $\theta_1 < \theta_2$, $N \cdot (p_B - p_A) \cdot (\theta_1 - \theta_2) < 0$.
Hence, $\Delta Z / \Delta n < 0$.
Therefore, Z monotonically decreases as n increases.

Bibliography

Bankers' Magazine: Journal of the Money Market, and Commercial Digest, London: Waterlow and Sons, Various Issues.

Bankers' Magazine and Statistical Register, New York: Homans Publishing Co., Various Issues.

Bagehot, Walter. *Lombard Street: A Description of the Money Market*, Westport: Hyperion Press, 1873.

Benston, George and Kaufman, George. "Risk and Solvency Regulation of Depository Institutions: Past Policies and Current Options," Staff Memoranda, Chicago: Federal Reserve Bank of Chicago, 1987.

Black, Fisher. "Banking and Interest Rates in a World without Money: The Effects of Uncontrolled Banking," *Journal of Bank Research*, 1970.

Bolles, Albert. *The National Bank Act and Its Judicial Meaning*, Philadelphia: George T. Bisel Co., 1910.

Brock, Phillip. "Financial Controls and Economic Liberalization in Latin America," Unpublished Manuscript, Duke University, 1985.

Bryant, John. "A Model of Reserves, Bank Runs, and Deposit Insurance," *Journal of Banking and Finance*, 1980.

Buchanan, James. "An Economic Theory of Club," *Economica*, 1965.

Burns, Helen. *The American Banking Community and New Deal Banking Reform: 1933 - 1935*, Westport: Greenwood Press, 1974.

Cass, David and Yaari, Menahem. "A Re-Examination of the Pure Consumption Loans model," *Journal of Political Economy*, 1966.

Chari, V. "Banking without Deposit Insurance or Bank Panics: Lesson from a Model of the U.S. National Banking System," *Quarterly Review*, Minneapolis: Federal Reserve Bank of Minneapolis, 1989.

Chari, V. and Jagannathan, Ravi. "Banking Panics, Information, and Rational Expectations Equilibrium," *Journal of Finance*, 1988.

Collman, Charles. *Our Mysterious Panics, 1830-1930*, New York: William Morrow and Co., 1931.

Commercial and Financial Chronicle and Hunt's Merchants' Magazine , New York: William B. Dona and Co., Various Issues.

Comptroller of the Currency. *Annual Report*, Washington: U.S. Government Printing Office, Various Issues.

Conant, Charles. *A History of Modern Banks of Issue*, New York: Knickerbocker Press, 1915.

Cothren, Richard. "Asymmetric Information and Optimal Bank Reserves," *Journal of Money, Credit, and Banking*, 1987.

Coway, Thomas Jr. and Patterson, Ernest. *The Operation of the New Bank Act*, Philadelphia: J.B. Lippincott Company, 1914.

Davis, Lance. "The Evolution of the American Capital Market, 1860-1940: A Case Study in Institutional Changes," in *Financial Innovation*, Edited by William L. Silber, Lexington: Lexington Books, 1975.

Diamond, Douglas. "Financial Intermediation and Delegated Monitoring," *Review of Economic Studies*, 1984.

Diamond, Douglas and Dybvig, Philip. "Bank Runs, Deposit Insurance, and Liquidity," *Journal of Political Economy*, 1983.

Diamond, Peter. "Credit in Search Equilibrium," in *Financial Constraints, Expectations, and Macroeconomics*, Edited by Meir Kohn and Sho-Chieh Tsiang, New York: Oxford University Press, 1988.

Donaldson, Glen. "Financial Panic, Liquidity and the Lender of Last Resort: A Strategic Analysis," Unpublished Manuscript, Brown University, 1988.

Dunbar, Charles. *Chapters on the Theory and History of Banking*, New York: The Knickerbocker Press, 1901.

Eames, Francis. *The New York Stock Exchange*, New York: Greenwood Press, 1894.

Eisenberg, Meyer. "The Current Status of the Regulation of Financial Services and Products in the United States: Developments and Trends," in *Changing Money: Financial Innovation in Developed Countries*, Edited by Marcello De Cecco, New York: Basil Blackwell Inc., 1987.

Fama, Eugene. "Banking in the Theory of Finance," *Journal of Monetary Economics*, 1980.

Federal Reserve Board. *Annual Report*, Washington: U.S. Government Printing Office, 1933a.

Federal Reserve Board, *Federal Reserve Bulletin*, Washington: U.S. Government Printing Office, 1933b.

Fischer, Gerald. *American Banking Structure*, New York: Columbia University Press, 1968.

Friedman, Milton. *A Program for Monetary Stability*, New York: Fordham University Press, 1959.

Friedman, Milton and Schwartz, Anna. *A Monetary History of the United States, 1867-1960*, Princeton: Princeton University Press, 1963.

Friedman, Milton and Schwartz, Anna. *Monetary Statistics of the United States*, New York: National Bureau of Economic Research, 1970.

Gennotte, Gerard. "Capital Controls and Bank Regulation," Discussion Series, Rome: Bank of Italy, 1987.

Goodhart, Charles. *The Evolution of Central Banks*, Cambridge: MIT Press, 1988.

Gorton, Gary. "Bank Suspension of Convertibility," *Journal of Monetary Economics*, 1985.

Greenfield, Robert and Yeager, Leland. "A *Laissez-Faire* Approach to Monetary Stability," *Journal of Money, Credit, and Banking*, 1983.

Gurley, J. and Shaw, E. *Money in a Theory of Finance*, Washington: Brookings Institution, 1960.

Hayek, F. *Denationalization of Money: An Analysis of the Theory and Practice of Concurrent Currencies*, Westminster: The Institute of Economic Affairs, 1976.

Hayek, F. "Toward a Free-Market Monetary System," *Journal of Libertarian Studies*, 1979.

Hirsch, Fred. "The Bagehot Problem," *The Manchester School of Economic and Social Studies*, 1977.

Jacklin, Charles. "Demand Deposits, Trading Restrictions, and Risk Sharing," in *Contractual Arrangements for Intertemporal Trade*, Edited by Edward Prescott and Neil Wallace, Minneapolis: University of Minnesota Press, 1987.

Kane, Thomas. *The Romance and Tragedy of Banking*, New York: Bankers Publishing Co., 1923.

Kareken, John and Wallace, Neil. "Deposit Insurance and Bank Regulation: A Partial Equilibrium Exposition," *Journal of Business*, 1978.

Kennedy, Susan. *The Banking Crisis of 1933*, Lexington: University Press of Kentucky, 1973.

Kindleberger, Charles. *Manias, Panics, and Crashes: A History of Financial Crises*, New York: Basic Books Inc., 1978.

Klein, Benjamin. "The Competitive Supply of Money," *Journal of Money, Credit, and Banking*, 1974.

Lightner, Otto. *The History of Business Depressions*, New York: Northeastern Press, 1922.

Lindley, Ernest. *The Roosevelt Revolution*, New York: Viking Press, 1933.

Marcus, Alan. "Deregulation and Bank Financial Policy," *Journal of Banking and Finance*, 1984.

Meltzer, Allan. "Monetary Reform in an Uncertain Environment," *Cato Journal*, 1983.

Merton, Robert. "On the Cost of Deposit Insurance When There Are Surveillance Costs," *Journal of Business*, 1978.

Mill, John Stuart. *Principles of Political Economy with Some of Their Applications to Social Philosophy*, London: Longmans, Green, and Co., 1848.

Moley, Raymond. *The First New Deal*, New York: Harcourt, Bruce and World Inc., 1966.

Nadler, Marcus and Bogen, Jules I. *The Banking Crisis: The End of an Epoch*, New York: Dodd, Mead and Company, 1933.

Nation. New York: E. L. Godkin & Co., Various Issues.

National Industrial Conference Board Inc. *The Banking Situation in the United States*, New York: Arno Press, 1980.

O'Connor, J. *The Banking Crisis and Recovery under the Roosevelt Administration*, Chicago: Callaghan and Company, 1938.

Postlewaite, Andrew and Vives, Xavier. "Bank Runs as an Equilibrium Phenomenon," *Journal of Political Economy*, 1987.

Ricardo, David. *On the Principles of Political Economy and Taxation*, Cambridge: Cambridge University, 1817.

Rolnick, Arthur and Weber, Warren. "Explaining the Demand for Free Bank Notes," Staff Report, Minneapolis: Federal Reserve Bank of Minneapolis, 1986.

Roosevelt, Franklin. *On Our Way*, New York: John Day Company, 1934.

Ross, Sheldon. *A First Course in Probability*, New York: Macmillan Publishing Company, 1984.

Rothschild, Michael and Stiglitz, Joseph. "Equilibrium in
    Competitive Insurance Markets: An Essay on the Economics
    of Imperfect Information," *Quarterly Journal of Economics*,
    1976.

Scott, James. "The Probability of Bankruptcy: A Comparison of
    Empirical Prediction and Theoretical Models," *Journal of
    Banking and Finance*, 1981.

Simons, Henry. *Economic Policy for a Free Society*, Chicago:
    University of Chicago Press, 1948.

Sinkley, Joseph. *Problem and Failed Institutions in the
    Commercial Banking Industry*, Greenwich: JAI Press Inc.,
    1979.

Smith, Adam. *An Inquiry into the Nature and Causes of the
    Wealth of Nations*, Chicago: University of Chicago Press,
    1776.

Smith, Bruce. "Private Information, the Real Bills Doctrine, and
    Quantity Theory: An Alternative Approach," in *Contractual
    Arrangements for Intertemporal Trade*, Edited by Edward
    Prescott and Neil Wallace, Minneapolis: University of
    Minnesota Press, 1987.

Sobel, Robert. *Panic on Wall Street: A History of American
    Financial Disasters*, New York: The Macmillan Company,
    1968.

Sprague, Irvine. *Bailout: An Insider's Account of Bank Failures
    and Rescues*, New York: Basic Books Inc., 1986.

Sprague, O. *History of Crisis under the National Banking System*, Washington: Government Printing Office, 1910.

Stiglitz, Joseph and Weiss, Andrew. "Credit Rationing in Market with Imperfect Information," *American Economic Review*, 1981.

Sullivan, Lawrence. *Prelude to Panic*, Washington: Statesman Press, 1936.

Upham, Cyril. and Lamke, Edwin. *Closed and Distressed Banks*, Washington: Brookings Institutions, 1934.

U.S. Department of Commerce. *Historical Statistics of the United States: 1789-1945*, Washington: Government Printing Office, 1949.

Vaubel, Roland. "Competing Currencies: The Case for Free Entry," *Cato Journal*, 1986.

Waldo, Douglas. "Bank Runs, the Deposit-Currency Ratio and the Interest Rate," *Journal of Monetary Economics*, 1985.

Wallace, Neil. "Another Attempt to Explain an Illiquid Banking System: The Diamond and Dybvig Model with Sequential Service Taken Seriously," *Quarterly Review*, Minneapolis: Federal Reserve Bank of Minneapolis, 1988.

White, Lawrence. "Competitive Money, Inside and Out," *Cato Journal*, 1983.

White, Lawrence. "Competitive Payment Systems and the Unit of Account," *American Economic Review*, 1984.

Williamson, Stephen. "Bank Failures, Financial Restrictions, and Aggregate Fluctuations: Canada and the United States, 1870-1913," *Quarterly Review*, Minneapolis: Federal Reserve Bank of Minneapolis, 1989.

Yeager, Leland. "Stable Money and Free Market Currencies," *Cato Journal*, 1983.

Index